THE BOOK OF
SAUCES

THE BOOK OF
SAUCES

GORDON GRIMSDALE

Photography by PER ERICSON

PUBLISHED BY
SALAMANDER BOOKS LIMITED
LONDON

Published 2000 by Salamander Books Limited
8 Blenheim Court, Brewery Road, London N7 9NT

By arrangement with Merehurst Fairfax
Ferry House 51-57 Lacy Road, London SW15 1PR

© Merehurst Fairfax and Gordon Grimsdale 1986

ISBN 1 84065 145 8

Editors: Susan Tomnay, Beverly LeBlanc, Chris Fayers
Designers: Susan Kinealy, Roger Daniels, Richard Slater,
         Stuart Willard
Food stylist: Jane Budgen assisted by Leanne Bennett
Photographer: Per Ericson
Typeset by Lineage
Colour separation by Photographics Ltd. London-Hong Kong
Printed in Spain

ACKNOWLEDGEMENTS
The Publisher would like to thank the following for their help
and advice:
Josiah Wedgwood & Sons, Sydney
Pillevuyt, Sydney
Incorporated Agences, Sydney

CONTENTS

INTRODUCTION

The word 'sauce' comes to us by a roundabout route from the feminine form of the Latin word 'salsa', meaning 'salted'. Perhaps the use of the feminine gender shows that in those far off Roman times a woman's place was in the kitchen. However, the day has long gone when using sauces is simply to flavour the main ingredient, as has the myth women should do all the work in kitchens.

Larousse defines sauce as 'liquid seasoning for food'. Webster, however, does more for the taste buds, listing sauce as 'a condiment or composition of condiments and appetizing ingredients eaten with food as a relish', or less appealing, 'a fluid, semifluid or sometimes semisolid accompaniment to solid food'. The great August Escoffier, 'King of Chiefs and the Chef of Kings', said sauces were the secret of the supremacy of French cuisine over all others.

Definitions, however, give no hint of the enormous importance of sauces in history. Sauce creation has produced vast gastronomic and culinary effects in making plain food more palatable, or, in earlier years, unpalatable food edible. A sentence describing the nature and function of sauces could never encompass the unlimited range of textures, flavours and aromas with which sauces can assault the senses and transform simple food into gourmet fare.

This book is an attempt to simplify sauce making and to remove some of the mystery that has shrouded even the basics. It is also aimed at improving both the taste and appearance of many different types of food, from savoury to sweet and spicy to tart. Follow the recipes and methods closely, but not too slavishly. Just remember, as long as certain basic rules are observed, there is always room for your own inventiveness to change a flavour subtly to suit your own taste buds.

BROWN STOCK

bouquet garni (6 fresh parsley sprigs, 2 fresh
    thyme sprigs and 2 bay leaves)
2 kg (4 lb) shin, shank or neck beef bones
3 litres (96 fl oz/12 cups) water
4 whole cloves
2 onions, halved crossways
2 carrots, coarsely chopped
1 small turnip, diced, if desired
2 celery stalks with leaves, coarsely sliced
1 garlic clove
1 scant teaspoon salt
10 black peppercorns

To make bouquet garni, tie together herb
sprigs with a piece of string or place in a
muslin bag; if string is used the bouquet
garni can be tied to the pan handles for
easy removal. Place bones and meat in a
roasting pan. Bake at 200C (400F/Gas
6), turning once, until brown.

Place the bones and any pieces of meat
left in roasting pan in a large saucepan or
casserole, and add water. Stick cloves
into onion halves and add to pan. Add all
remaining ingredients, except salt and
peppercorns. Bring to the boil over
moderate heat, then add salt and
peppercorns. Skim surface as necessary.
Lower heat and simmer, uncovered, 3½
to 4 hours.

Remove bouquet garni and pour through
a fine strainer; cool. Remove any fat that
solidifies on surface. Cover tightly and
store in refrigerator for up to 1 week.

Makes about 2 litres (64 fl oz/8 cups).

WHITE STOCK

750 g (1½ lb) veal or chicken bones, or a
    combination with any meat attached to them
3 litres (96 fl oz/12 cups) water
4 whole cloves
2 onions, halved crossways
2 leeks, coarsely chopped
2 small carrots, coarsely chopped
1 celery stalk, coarsely sliced
bouquet garni (4 fresh parsley sprigs, 1 fresh
    thyme sprig, 1 bay leaf, page 8)
8 black peppercorns

Place meat and bones in a large saucepan
or casserole, cover with water and let
stand for 1 hour. Bring water to the boil
over high heat, skim the surface. Lower
heat and simmer until liquid is clear.

Stick cloves into onion halves and add to
pan. Add remaining ingredients. Bring
to the boil again, cover, lower heat and
simmer very gently for 3 hours, skimming
as necessary.

Remove bouquet garni and pour through
a fine strainer, then refrigerate until cool.
Spoon off any fat that solidified on
surface. Cover tightly and store in the
refrigerator up to 2 weeks.

Makes about 2 litres (64 fl oz/8 cups).

FISH STOCK

1 kg (2 lb) fish bones and trimmings
500 g (1 lb) white fish, such as cod
1 medium onion, thinly sliced crossways
1 leek, thinly sliced
1 carrot, thinly sliced
2 tablespoons lemon juice
bouquet garni (10 fresh parsley sprigs, 1 fresh
   thyme sprig and 1 bay leaf, page 8)
2 litres (64 fl oz/8 cups) water
12 black peppercorns
½ teaspoon salt

Place all ingredients in a large saucepan
or casserole over moderate heat. Bring to
the boil, lower temperature and simmer
gently, uncovered, for 30 minutes.

Skim surface as required during cooking.
Pour through a fine strainer, then cool.
Cover tightly and store in the refrigerator
for up to 2 days.

Makes about 1.2 litres (40 fl oz/5 cups).

VARIATION:
For a rich stock use three-quarters water
and one-quarter dry white wine. Strain
liquid, then return to the cleaned pan
and boil over high heat until reduced to
two-thirds.

BASIC ROUX

A roux is made by combining equal amounts melted butter and flour with a liquid. Recipes will specify the exact quantities but the golden rule is to use equal amounts of flour and butter. Melt butter in a heavy-based saucepan over moderate heat.

Add flour all at once; blend in, stirring constantly for 3 to 10 minutes (see below). Remove from heat and gradually add some of the liquid. Return to heat; whisk constantly until all the liquid is absorbed and sauce is smooth and lump-free. Continue until all liquid is used, boiling and thickening sauce after each addition.

The colour of the roux is determined by how long the flour is cooked; *roux blanc* is white and takes about 3 minutes; *roux blond* is a pale, sandy colour and takes about 5 minutes; *roux brun* is cooked about 10 minutes until it becomes brown.

VELOUTÉ SAUCE

750 ml (24 fl oz/3 cups) White Stock, page 9
45 g (1½ oz) butter
45 g (1½ oz/3 tablespoons) plain flour
White pepper and salt

Warm the stock in a heavy-based saucepan over moderate heat.

Melt butter in another heavy-based saucepan. Stir in flour and cook about 3 minutes, until bubbly. Gradually add warmed stock, whisking constantly. Cook, uncovered, at a slow simmer 50 minutes to 1 hour, stirring occasionally, until reduced by one-third.

Skim surface as necessary during cooking. Pour through a fine strainer. Keep hot in top of a double boiler until ready to use. Serve with grilled chicken breasts (fillets) or lightly-cooked green vegetables.

Makes about 500 ml (16 fl oz/2 cups).

VARIATIONS
Chicken Velouté Sauce: Replace White Stock with chicken stock.

Fish Velouté Sauce: Replace White Stock with Fish Stock, page 10.

Veal Velouté Sauce: Replace White Stock with veal stock.

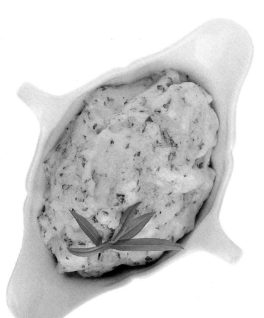

──── BÉARNAISE SAUCE ────

1 spring onion, or 1 small onion, finely chopped
2 sprigs fresh chervil
2 teaspoons finely chopped fresh tarragon, or
    1 teaspoon dried tarragon
At least 4 crushed black peppercorns, or more
    according to taste
2 tablespoons white wine vinegar
2 tablespoons dry white wine
3 egg yolks
180 g (6 oz) firm butter, cut in pieces
Salt
Cayenne pepper
Finely chopped fresh tarragon or parsley, if
    desired

In a small saucepan, combine spring onion, chervil, tarragon, pepper, vinegar and wine. Cook over moderate heat until liquid is reduced by half.

Place egg yolks in top half of a double boiler over barely simmering water. Pour onion mixture through a fine strainer into egg yolks; whisk until blended. Do not allow water to boil or touch bottom of top half of boiler.

Add butter, piece by piece, whisking constantly. Make sure each piece is melted and absorbed before adding next piece. The sauce should be smooth like mayonnaise. Adjust seasoning with salt and cayenne. Stir in chopped herb, if desired, and serve warm with roast beef, steaks, chicken or fish.

Makes about 500 ml (16 fl oz/2 cups).

MAYONNAISE

2 egg yolks
Salt and white pepper
1 teaspoon Dijon or dried mustard, if desired
1 teaspoon white wine or tarragon vinegar, or
    lemon juice
About 250 ml (8 fl oz/1 cup) olive or vegetable oil

Place egg yolks in a bowl with salt and pepper, mustard, if desired and ⅛ teaspoon vinegar or lemon juice.

Whisking constantly with a wire whisk, add oil drop by drop at first, then in a steady trickle until the mayonnaise is thick. Add remaining vinegar and adjust seasoning, if desired; stir again.

Makes about 250 ml (8 fl oz/1 cup).

BLENDER MAYONNAISE
Place first three ingredients and ⅛ teaspoon vinegar or lemon juice in a blender or bowl of food processor fitted with a metal blade. With motor running, add oil drop by drop through hole in lid, then in a steady trickle until the desired consistency is achieved. Add remaining vinegar. Do not overprocess or it will be too thick.

Makes about 250 ml (8 fl oz/1 cup).

Note: If you want to store either version, stir in 1 tablespoon boiling water to prevent curdling. Do not refrigerate; store in screw-top jars in a cool place, such as a larder or store cupboard.

Mayonnaise Variations

CURRIED MAYONNAISE

1 garlic clove, crushed
250 ml (8 fl oz/1 cup) Mayonnaise, page 14
1 teaspoon curry powder, or to taste
1 teaspoon very finely chopped fresh coriander or
    parsley or ½ teaspoon coriander powder

Add garlic to Mayonnaise; sprinkle in curry powder, stirring well. Fold in coriander or parsley. Serve with cold cooked chicken or fish, such as poached salmon.
Makes 250 ml (8 fl oz/1 cup).

HORSERADISH MAYONNAISE

4 tablespoons very finely chopped grated fresh
    horseradish, or less according to taste
250 ml (8 fl oz/1 cup) Mayonnaise, page 14

Stir together horseradish and Mayonnaise. Serve with hot or cold roast beef and poached or smoked fish.
Makes 250 ml (8 fl oz/1 cup).

MINT MAYONNAISE

½ teaspoon boiling water
3 teaspoons finely chopped fresh mint
¼ teaspoon sugar
2 tablespoons white wine vinegar, warmed
250 ml (8 fl oz/1 cup) Mayonnaise, page 14

In a small bowl, sprinkle water on mint and sugar. Crush with back of spoon to extract as much mint flavour as possible. Add vinegar; stir this mixture through Mayonnaise. Serve with leftover lamb, with crisp vegetables as a dip and with salads as a dressing.
Makes 250 ml (8 fl oz/1 cup).

SAUCE ESPAGNOLE

60 g (2 oz) butter
60 g (2 oz/½ cup) plain flour
1.2 litres (40 fl oz/5 cups) Brown stock, page 8,
   warm
2 tablespoons bacon fat
1 small onion, finely chopped
1 celery stalk, finely chopped
1 small carrot, thinly sliced
Bouquet garni (1 sprig fresh thyme, 1 bay leaf,
   6 sprigs fresh parsley tied together, page 8)
Salt and pepper
Strips of orange rind, to garnish

In a medium heavy-based saucepan melt
60 g (2 oz) butter over very low heat. Add
flour and cook about 10 minutes, stirring
constantly, until roux turns a rich peanut
butter colour: the slower the cooking the
better the flavour.

Whisking constantly, gradually add
stock; use a whisk to blend thoroughly.
Bring to the boil gently over moderate
heat, then lower heat to low and cook,
uncovered, for about 30 minutes.

Meanwhile, in a small saucepan, melt remaining butter and bacon fat. Add vegetables and brown, stirring constantly,
over moderate heat. Add contents of this
pan and bouquet garni to the stock.
Slowly simmer, uncovered, over low heat
for 1½ to 2 hours. Skim surface as
necessary. Season to taste. Remove
bouquet garni and pour through a fine
strainer; cool. Spoon off any fat that
solidifies on surface. Garnish.

Makes about 1.2 litres (40 fl oz/5 cups).

QUICK BROWN SAUCE

60 g (2 oz) butter
2 tablespoons finely chopped onion
1 tablespoon finely chopped celery
1 tablespoon finely chopped carrot
Bouquet garni (4 sprigs fresh parsley, 1 bay leaf,
　　1 sprig fresh thyme tied together, page 8)
½ teaspoon salt
Pepper
60 g (2 oz/½ cup) plain flour
250 ml (8 fl oz/1 cup) Brown Stock, page 8

In a small, heavy-based saucepan, melt butter. Add chopped vegetables and bouquet garni. Sauté gently, stirring often, for 5 to 6 minutes, until vegetables begin to brown.

Add salt and pepper. Stir in flour. Cook, stirring, for 5 to 6 minutes. Warm stock in a separate saucepan, then add to vegetables. Stir constantly over a moderate heat until sauce boils. When thick, simmer for about 5 minutes.

Remove bouquet garni and pour through a fine strainer. Serve hot with grilled lamb chops, pork chops or steaks.

Makes about 250 ml (8 fl oz/1 cup).

Note: If not using at once, keep in top of a double boiler over simmering water. Adding more stock will produce a thinner sauce.

Béchamel Sauce

750 ml (24 fl oz/3 cups) milk
90 g (3 oz) butter
2 tablespoons grated onion
90 g (3 oz/¾ cup) plain flour
2 sprigs fresh parsley
6 white peppercorns
Pinch of freshly grated nutmeg
Salt

Warm milk in a saucepan over very low heat. Meanwhile, melt butter in another heavy-based saucepan and add onion.

Sauté onion until golden; do not allow to turn brown. Stir in flour and cook over low heat for 3 minutes or until bubbly. Gradually add milk, whisking constantly.

Cook until sauce thickens; add parsley, peppercorns, nutmeg and salt. Keep heat very low and continue cooking 20 to 25 minutes, uncovered, stirring frequently. The sauce should be thick and creamy; thin with extra milk, if desired. Pour through a fine strainer.

Makes about 750 ml (24 fl oz/3 cups).

Note: If made in advance, float 1 tablespoon melted butter on top. To serve, re-heat in top of double boiler over simmering water; beat in butter.

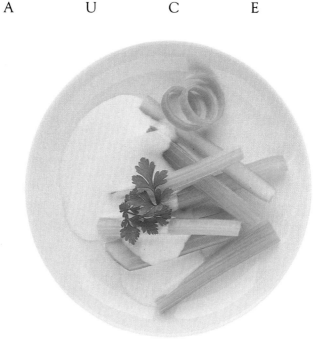

WHITE SAUCE

500 ml (16 fl oz/2 cups) milk
60 g (2 oz) butter
60 g (2 oz/½ cup) plain flour
Salt and white pepper

Warm milk in a saucepan over low heat. In a seperate heavy-based saucepan melt butter. Add flour all at once and cook about 3 minutes, without browning.

Whisking constantly, gradually add milk.

Continue whisking until sauce thickens; cook 2 to 3 minutes over low heat, stirring occasionally, until the consistency is rich and creamy. Season. Serve hot with lightly cooked vegetables or use as a base for other sauces.

Makes about 500 ml (16 fl oz/2 cups).

Note: More or less milk will produce a thinner or thicker sauce. Keep warm, if necessary, in top of double boiler over simmering water, but do not cover because the steam will thin sauce.

TOMATO SAUCE 1

150 ml (5 fl oz/²⁄₃ cup) Brown Stock, page 8
1 kg (2 lb) ripe tomatoes, peeled, quartered
8 fresh basil leaves, or 1 teaspoon dried basil
Salt and pepper
Sugar, if desired

In a large saucepan, add stock to tomatoes.

Add basil and cook until tomatoes are reduced to a pulp; this may take 35 to 45 minutes, depending on ripeness.

Purée in a food processor or blender. Add salt and pepper and a little sugar if tomatoes are too tart. Serve hot with grilled sausages or steaks.

Makes about 600 ml (20 fl oz/2½ cups).

TOMATO SAUCE 2

1 kg (2 lb) ripe tomatoes
1½ tablespoons olive oil
125 g (4 oz) onion, finely chopped
1 celery stalk, finely chopped
2 tablespoons tomato purée (paste)
1 bay leaf
6 fresh basil leaves, or 1 teaspoon dried basil
1 teaspoon sugar
1 teaspoon salt
Pepper

Dip tomatoes in boiling water to split the skin, then spear with a fork and skin. Quarter tomatoes and set aside.

In a heavy-based saucepan, heat oil over a low heat. Sauté onions and celery until onions are golden. Add tomatoes and any juice, tomato purée (paste), bay leaf, basil, sugar, and salt and pepper.

Bring to the boil. Lower heat and simmer gently, uncovered, for 45 minutes, stirring occasionally. Remove bay leaf and discard. Serve hot with freshly-cooked pasta.

Makes about 600 ml (20 fl oz/2½ cups).

HOLLANDAISE SAUCE

3 egg yolks, at room temperature
1 tablespoon water
2 teaspoons lemon juice
180 g (6 oz) butter, diced, at room temperature
Salt and white pepper
Paprika or cayenne pepper, if desired

In top of a double boiler over low heat, whisk egg yolks, water and lemon juice until fluffy. Check water in bottom of double boiler so it doesn't touch bottom of top half or boil.

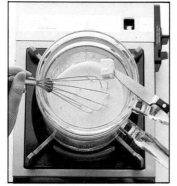

Add butter, piece by piece, making sure each piece is incorporated before adding the next; continue until all butter has been used.

Season with salt and pepper, sprinkling with paprika or cayenne pepper, if desired. Pour into a warm serving dish and serve at once with steamed asparagus, lightly cooked fresh vegetables or poached seafood, such as salmon.

Makes about 250 ml (8 fl oz/1 cup).

Note: If sauce starts to curdle, add 1 tablespoon boiling water, whisking constantly. It is also possible to whisk another egg yolk in a bowl and whisk the curdled mixture into the egg yolk; return to double boiler.

SAUCE ROBERT

2 tablespoons butter
2 medium onions, finely chopped
2 tablespoons plain flour
125 ml (4 fl oz/½ cup) dry white wine
250 ml (8 fl oz/1 cup) Brown Stock, page 8
½ teaspoon red wine vinegar
1 teaspoon Dijon mustard
1 small dill pickle

In a moderate heavy-based saucepan, melt butter. Add onions and sauté until soft and golden brown. Remove onions with a slotted spoon and set aside. Add flour and stir to make roux, cooking 3 to 4 minutes, until bubbly.

Return onions to the pan. Add wine and stock. Bring just to the boil over moderate heat, stirring constantly. Reduce heat and simmer for 20 minutes, uncovered.

Slice pickle, then finely chop. Add vinegar, mustard and pickle to sauce and cook 1 minute. Serve hot with grilled pork chops or roast duck.

Makes about 250 ml (8 fl oz/1 cup).

MORNAY SAUCE

3 egg yolks, lightly beaten
60 ml (2 fl oz/¼ cup) double (thickened) cream
500 ml (16 fl oz/2 cups) Béchamel Sauce, page
   18, kept warm
30 g (1 oz) Parmesan cheese, freshly-grated

In a heavy-based saucepan, mix together egg yolks and cream. Add Béchamel Sauce over low heat, stirring constantly, until just boiling.

Remove from heat and mix in cheese; stir to melt. Serve hot with freshly steamed vegetables or cooked chicken or fish.

Makes about 500 ml (16 fl oz/2 cups).

RICH MORNAY SAUCE

500 ml (16 fl oz/2 cups) Béchamel Sauce, page
   18, kept warm
90 g (3 oz) butter
75 g (2½ oz)/Parmesan or Gruyere cheese, grated

In a heavy-based saucepan, place Béchamel Sauce and keep warm over low heat. Just before serving, stir in butter and cheese; continue stirring until melted.

Makes about 500 ml (16 fl oz/2 cups).

SAUCE VINAIGRETTE

60 ml (2 fl oz/¼ cup) red or white wine vinegar
¼ teaspoon salt
¼ teaspoon freshly ground pepper
½ teaspoon prepared or Dijon mustard, if desired
125 ml (4 fl oz/½ cup) olive, or vegetable oil

Use a whisk to blend all the ingredients, except the oil, together in a bowl.

Add the oil slowly, whisking continuously. When it has all been absorbed, taste the sauce; some may find the balance of ingredients too oily, especially if the vinegar is mild.

Adjust with extra vinegar, salt or pepper to suit taste. Serve with salads or crudités.

Makes about 180 ml (6 fl oz/¾ cup).

Note: Store up to 1 month in a screw-top jar in a refrigerator; shake before using.

APPLE SAUCE

500 g (1 lb) cooking apples
3 tablespoons butter
2 tablespoons lemon juice
1 whole clove
Sugar, to taste
Pinch of ground cinnamon

Peel, core and slice the apples.

In a saucepan place the sliced apples; add butter, lemon juice, clove and sugar, if needed. Cover and cook over very low heat until apples are soft. Remove the clove.

Use a fork to beat the mixture gently until it is fluffy. Add a pinch of cinnamon. Serve with roast pork, duck or goose.

Makes about 500 ml (16 fl oz/2 cups).

PORT & RASPBERRY SAUCE

180 g (6 oz/½ cup) redcurrant jelly
60 ml (2 fl oz/¼ cup) port wine
2 teaspoons lemon juice
375 g (12 oz) raspberries, fresh or thawed
2 teaspoons arrowroot
Pepper

Spoon measured jelly into a heavy-based saucepan. Add port and lemon juice; stir over low heat until jelly melts and ingredients are combined.

Reserve a few raspberries for garnish; press remainder through fine strainer. Add puree to redcurrant mixture in saucepan and heat gently.

In a small bowl, mix arrowroot with a little of the warm sauce. Return to saucepan and cook, stirring, until sauce thickens, then add pepper. Serve hot with reserved raspberries with roast game or vegetables wrapped in filo pastry.

Makes about 250 ml (8 fl oz/1 cup).

Note: If using frozen raspberries, drain well after thawing or sauce will be thin.

REDCURRANT SAUCE

250 g (8 oz/²⁄₃ cup) redcurrant jelly
75 ml (2½ fl oz/¹⁄₃ cup) orange juice
1 small bunch fresh mint leaves, finely chopped
Strips of orange rind, to garnish

In a small saucepan, melt jelly over low heat.

Remove from heat and stir in orange juice and mint. Garnish with strips of orange rind, if desired.

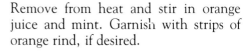

Alternatively, jelly can be placed in a microwave-safe bowl and covered with cling film, then microwaved at high for 1½ minutes, until melted. Stir in orange juice and mint.

Makes about 250 ml (8 fl oz/1 cup).

SAUCE VÉRONIQUE

250 ml (8 fl oz/1 cup) fish poaching liquid, or
    Fish Stock, page 10
60 ml (2 fl oz/¼ cup) dry white wine
1 tablespoon brandy
1 tablespoon finely chopped spring onion
1 teaspoon cornflour
2 teaspoons cold water
125 ml (4 fl oz/½ cup) double (thickened) cream
Salt and white pepper
16 seedless green grapes
2 tablespoons butter, in small pieces

Boil poaching liquid, wine, brandy and
spring onion together in a medium
heavy-based saucepan until the liquid is
reduced to about 125 ml (4 fl oz/½ cup).
Strain and return to pan.

Blend cornflour with water; add to
saucepan over moderate heat. Cook until
bubbly. Stir in cream. Cook, stirring
until sauce boils. Add salt and pepper to
taste.

Add grapes. As soon as the grapes are
warmed through, add butter. Blend
thoroughly but gently. Serve hot with
poached fish.

Makes about 250 ml (8 fl oz/1 cup).

Prune Sauce

200 g (7 oz) stoned prunes
2 tablespoons lemon juice
1 tablespoon finely grated lemon rind
8 whole cloves
Pinch of ground cinnamon
Pinch of ground allspice
½ teaspoon freshly grated nutmeg
About 250 ml (8 fl oz/1 cup) water
125 g (4 oz/½ cup) sugar
About 125 ml (4 fl oz/½ cup) red wine vinegar

Mix prunes, lemon juice and rind with cloves, cinnamon, allspice and nutmeg. Transfer to a heavy-based saucepan.

Add just enough water to cover and heat until simmering; cook slowly for about 15 minutes or until prunes are soft; stirring occasionally. When liquid has reduced to about half, take off heat and remove cloves.

Pass through a fine strainer or purée in a food processor. Return to saucepan. Add sugar and vinegar. Cook over low heat, stirring until smooth and warmed through. Serve with roast pork.

Makes about 500 ml (16 fl oz/2 cups).

BIGARADE SAUCE

1½ tablespoons plain flour
375 ml (12 fl oz/1½ cups) hot water
Peeled rind of 2 oranges
1 tablespoon Curaçao, if desired
Juice of 1 orange
2 teaspoons lemon juice
Salt and pepper

This sauce is traditionally served with roast duck. When duck has been roasted, remove from the roasting pan and keep warm. Pour off any fat remaining in the pan, leaving cooking juices.

Sprinkle on flour and stir to combine with juices. Keep stirring over moderate heat until flour is browned; add the water and bring to the boil, stirring constantly. Lower heat and simmer 5 minutes, stirring occasionally.

Meanwhile, cut orange rind into thin matchstick strips and boil gently for a few minutes to remove the bitterness. Drain. Add strips of rind to the roasting pan. Cook 5 minutes over gentle heat until the rind is soft; add the Curaçao, if desired. Stir in orange and lemon juices and adjust the seasoning with salt and pepper. Serve hot with the duck.

Makes about 500 ml (16 fl oz/2 cups).

RAISIN SAUCE

30 g (1 oz/¼ cup) plain flour
1½ tablespoons light brown sugar
1½ tablespoons dry mustard
Salt and white pepper
375 ml (12 fl oz/1½ cups) water
2 tablespoons white wine vinegar
1 tablespoon lemon juice
60 g (2 oz/⅓ cup) seedless raisins
2 tablespoons butter

Place the first four ingredients in a heavy-based saucepan; stir to blend.

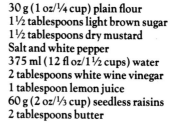

Bring water to the boil in a separate saucepan and whisk into dry ingredients, a little at a time, stirring constantly, to produce a smooth sauce. Add vinegar and lemon juice and simmer over moderate heat for 7 to 8 minutes.

Add raisins. Lower heat to low and cook for 3 minutes more, or until raisins are soft and plump. Just before serving, stir in the butter until melted. Serve hot with boiled ham.

Makes about 440 ml (14 fl oz/1¾ cups).

– ORANGE & GRAPEFRUIT SAUCE –

2 tablespoons unsalted butter
250 g (8oz) fish bones and trimmings
2 spring onions, coarsely chopped
1 small celery stalk, chopped
250 ml (8 fl oz/1 cup) dry white wine
1 large orange, peeled
1 large grapefruit, peeled
315 ml (10 fl oz/1¼ cups) double (thickened)
   cream

In a heavy-based saucepan over moderate heat, melt butter; add fish bones, trimmings, onions and celery. Sauté over moderate heat for a few minutes, stirring occasionally, until onion is golden and the celery is softening.

Add wine. Simmer for 15 to 20 minutes. If liquid reduces too much, add a little water. Strain stock into a bowl; discard bones and vegetables.

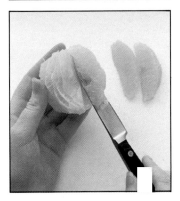

Segment orange and grapefruit. Return stock to saucepan and add orange and grapefruit segments; heat through over moderate heat. Lower heat, add cream and salt and pepper. Serve hot with grilled or poached fish.

Makes about 500 ml (16 fl oz/2 cups).

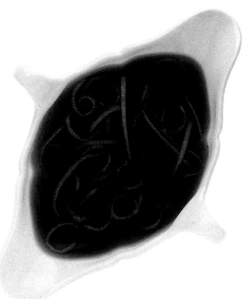

CUMBERLAND SAUCE

1 orange
1 lemon
125 ml (4 fl oz/½ cup) port wine
250 g (8 oz/⅔ cup) redcurrant jelly
1 tablespoon red wine vinegar
Pinch of cayenne pepper
Salt
½ teaspoon prepared mustard, if desired
6 glacé cherries, finely chopped

Peel orange and lemon carefully so that no white pith is removed. Cut the rind into julienne strips. Place strips in a saucepan and cover with water. Cook for about 5 minutes. Strain and set strips aside.

In a medium saucepan, add juice from the lemon and orange and all remaining ingredients, except cherries. Add drained orange and lemon strips. The mustard, if desired, will add extra sharpness.

Boil gently for about 5 minutes over high heat. Remove from heat and cool. Add the cherries. Serve cold with ham or other meat and game.

Makes about 375 ml (12 fl oz/1½ cups).

TERIYAKI SAUCE

1 tablespoon grated onion
3 small garlic cloves, crushed
1 tablespoon grated fresh root ginger
Salt
250 ml (8 fl oz/1 cup) soy sauce
1 teaspoon sesame oil
125 ml (4 fl oz/½ cup) Japanese saké, or dry
  sherry
60 g (2 oz/⅓ cup) light brown sugar
1 kg (2 lb) chicken or fish pieces, to serve

Place all ingredients in a small saucepan and warm gently over moderate heat, stirring until sugar has dissolved.

Strain through fine muslin, if desired, but the sauce is excellent as it is – the small flakes of onion, garlic and ginger give it body.

This sauce can also be used as a marinade. Skewer pieces of chicken or fish and place in a glass bowl. Cover with sauce and set aside at least 3 to 4 hours, turning occasionally. Grill or barbecue the chicken or fish, basting frequently with sauce. Warm any remaining sauce and serve with cooked chicken or fish.

Makes about 375 ml (12 fl oz/1½ cups).

ITALIAN SEAFOOD SAUCE

180 ml (6 fl oz/¾ cup) dry white wine
125 g (4 oz) raw prawns
125 g (4 oz) clams, in the shell, if desired
12 small mussels, in the shell
Pepper
Tabasco sauce
75 ml (2½ fl oz/⅓ cup) olive oil
2 garlic cloves, lightly crushed
½ teaspoon dried oregano
½ tablespoon chopped fresh coriander
60 ml (2 fl oz/¼ cup) brandy
125 g (4 oz) cleaned squid bodies, cut in rings
250 ml (8 fl oz/1 cup) Tomato Sauce 1, page 20
250 g (8 oz) firm white fish, such as cod, chopped

In a large saucepan, heat 60 ml (2 fl oz/¼ cup) wine. Add prawns and unopened clams, if desired, and mussels. Add pepper and a few drops of Tabasco sauce. Bring to the boil, stirring.

When mussel and clam shells open, remove and reserve; discard any which do not open. Remove prawns and reserve. Cool slightly, then peel. Strain and reserve cooking liquid.

In another saucepan, heat oil and garlic until golden; remove and discard. Add herbs and remaining wine and brandy. Simmer about 3 minutes. Add squid and simmer for 4 minutes, stirring; remove and reserve. Add Tomato Sauce and bring to the boil; add reserved cooking liquid and white fish. Lower heat; simmer 10 minutes until fish is almost cooked through. Return shellfish and squid. Lower heat and cook 1 to 2 minutes.
Makes 500 ml (16 fl oz/2 cups).

BLACK BEAN SAUCE

1 tablespoon canned black beans
2 small garlic cloves, crushed
1 teaspoon sugar
2 tablespoons vegetable oil
6 tablespoons water
1 tablespoon soy sauce
1 teaspoon cornflour
2 teaspoons water
2 large onions, sliced

Wash black beans in cold water, then strain.

Place beans on flat surface, add garlic and sprinkle over sugar. Mash with a fork to blend thoroughly. Heat 1 tablespoon oil in large frying pan over moderate heat and stir-fry bean mixture for 1 minute; stir in water and soy sauce. Bring to the boil, then lower heat and simmer 2 minutes. Meanwhile, mix cornflour with 2 teaspoons water. Stir into bean mixture; bring to the boil and cook for 1 minute. Remove from frying pan and keep warm.

Heat remaining 1 tablespoon oil; add onions and cook about 5 minutes, until soft and golden. Return bean mixture and stir-fry until heated through. Serve hot with rice and stir-fried beef.

Makes 125 ml (4 fl oz/½ cup).

ITALIAN GREEN SAUCE

30 g (1 oz/¼ cup) fresh white breadcrumbs
2 tablespoons white wine vinegar
1 hard-boiled egg yolk
15 g (½ oz/¾ cup) finely chopped fresh parsley
2 anchovy fillets, drained and coarsely chopped
1 garlic clove, finely chopped
1 teaspoon finely chopped capers
About 250 ml (8 fl oz/1 cup) olive oil
Salt and pepper

In a small bowl, soak the breadcrumbs in the vinegar.

Meanwhile, place egg yolk in a medium bowl. Mash with the parsley, anchovies, garlic and capers. Squeeze vinegar out of the breadcrumbs and add the breadcrumbs to egg mixture.

Add oil and blend until sauce is smooth and creamy. Add salt and pepper to taste. Let stand for 1 to 2 hours. Serve cold with boiled meat or steamed fish.

Makes about 250 ml (8 fl oz/1 cup).

FRENCH GREEN SAUCE

15 g (½ oz/¾ cup) coarsely chopped fresh
    chervil
15 g (½ oz/¾ cup) coarsely chopped fresh
    parsley
15 g (½ oz/¾ cup) coarsely chopped fresh
    tarragon
15 g (½ oz/¾ cup) coarsely chopped watercress
    leaves
4 spinach leaves, chopped
250 ml (8 fl oz/1 cup) Mayonnaise, page 14
Few drops of onion juice
8 capers, drained and finely chopped, if desired
1 teaspoon chopped fresh parsley

Wash herbs and spinach well. Place into
a medium saucepan of boiling water and
cook for 1 minute; strain.

Press with a wooden spoon in a fine
strainer to extract all liquid, reserving
liquid. Discard cooked leaves. Set liquid
aside until cool.

Carefully add liquid to Mayonnaise, taking care not to let it curdle. Add 2 to 3
drops onion juice and the capers, if
desired. Cool, then transfer to a
sauce-boat and garnish with chopped
parsley. Serve with cooked salmon or
trout.

Makes 250 ml (8 fl oz/1 cup).

— GREEN PEPPERCORN SAUCE 1 —

2 tablespoons butter
1 spring onion, finely chopped
2 tablespoons brandy
250 ml (8 fl oz/1 cup) Brown Stock, page 8
1 tablespoon beurre manié (made from
   ½ tablespoon room temperature butter,
   blended with ½ tablespoon plain flour)
1 teaspoon green peppercorns, lightly crushed
2 teaspoons green peppercorns, uncrushed
3 tablespoons double (thickened) cream
Salt and pepper

In a heavy-based saucepan, melt butter and sweat onion over moderate heat until soft. Increase heat slightly; add brandy. Add stock and stir while bringing to the boil. Continue cooking until the liquid is reduced to a little less than 250 ml (8 fl oz/1 cup). Remove onions with a slotted spoon. Bring back to the boil.

Add beurre manié a little at a time, using a whisk to blend well with the liquid.

When sauce begins to thicken, add crushed and uncrushed peppercorns. Lower heat and simmer gently for about 5 minutes. Add cream; stir well and season. Serve hot with pan-fried or grilled steaks.

Makes about 250 ml (8 fl oz/1 cup).

Note: The best peppercorns for this purpose are packed in water and sold in bottles. Remove them from the water and allow to dry before use.

— GREEN PEPPERCORN SAUCE 2 —

½ teaspoon green peppercorns, uncrushed
60 ml (2 fl oz/¼ cup) milk
180 ml (6 fl oz/¾ cup) poaching liquid, from fish
  or chicken, or White Stock, page 9
75 ml (2½ fl oz/⅓ cup) dry white wine
1 tablespoon Cognac
2 teaspoons Dijon mustard
60 ml (2 fl oz/¼ cup) double (thickened) cream
1 scant teaspoon green peppercorns, crushed
Salt

Place green peppercorns in a small
strainer; strain, then set aside on
absorbent kitchen paper to dry.

In a heavy-based saucepan, add milk to
poaching liquid; bring to the boil. In
another small, heavy-based saucepan
boil wine and Cognac. When milk
mixture has reduced to less than half, add
wine and brandy.

Continue cooking over low heat; add
mustard and cream. Stir constantly for 1
to 2 minutes. Add crushed and
uncrushed peppercorns. Heat through,
then serve hot with fish fillets or chicken
breasts (fillets).

Makes about 250 ml (8 fl oz/1 cup).

AÏOLI SAUCE

6 medium garlic cloves
Salt
2 egg yolks
About 125 ml (4 fl oz/½ cup) olive oil
2 teaspoons lemon juice or tarragon vinegar
Pepper

Press the garlic cloves through a garlic press into a bowl. Beat to a paste with the salt. Add egg yolks, one at a time, and beat until well combined.

Slowly drip in oil, as for mayonnaise, whisking constantly. When sauce begins to thicken, stir in lemon juice, and continue to add oil, gradually increasing to a steady trickle. Enough oil has been added when sauce becomes really thick.

Add pepper; stir well. Serve sauce with crudités or cold meats.

Makes about 250 ml (8 fl oz/1 cup).

Note: Do not refrigerate any leftover Aïoli; place in a screw-top jar and leave in a cool place, such as a larder.

BAGNA CAUDA

6 flat canned anchovy fillets, in oil, drained
3 large garlic cloves, coarsely chopped
Salt
60 ml (2 fl oz/¼ cup) olive oil
6 tablespoons butter
Pepper

Crush anchovy fillets and garlic in a pestle and mortar until they form a paste. A little salt sprinkled over the garlic will help.

Heat oil and butter in a small heavy-based saucepan and add the anchovy-garlic mixture, stirring to combine well.

Add pepper and transfer to a heatproof serving dish or fondue pot. Serve hot with crudités or Italian bread sticks for dipping into the sauce.

Makes about 250 ml (8 fl oz/1 cup).

Note: If possible, try to keep hot over a flame.

ANDALUSIAN SAUCE

1 red pepper (capsicum)
250 ml (8 fl oz/1 cup) Velouté Sauce, page 12,
    either kept warm or cold
1 tablespoon finely chopped fresh parsley
1 tablespoon finely chopped pimiento
2 tablespoons tomato purée (paste)
1 teaspoon lemon juice

Char pepper under grill until black all over. Set aside until cool enough to handle. Peel off skin.

Cut pepper into lengthways strips, then finely dice.

In a bowl, combine all ingredients. Serve with cold roast meats, chicken or hard-boiled eggs.

Makes about 250 ml (8 fl oz/1 cup).

Note: If you do not have time to make Velouté Sauce, substitute 250 ml (8 fl oz/1 cup) Mayonnaise, page 14.

—————— Smetana Sauce ——————

1 small onion
2 tablespoons butter
75 ml (2½ fl oz/⅓ cup) dry white wine
1 teaspoon plain flour
250 ml (8 fl oz/1 cup) soured cream
2 tablespoons lemon juice
Salt and pepper

Peel and finely chop onion. In a small, heavy-based saucepan, melt butter over low heat. Sauté onion until golden brown.

Add wine, increase heat and bring to the boil. Continue boiling until liquid is reduced to about half its original volume.

Stir flour into soured cream. Slowly add soured cream to hot liquid stirring constantly. Bring back to the boil briefly. Remove from heat and pour through a fine strainer; discard onion. Add lemon juice and season to taste with salt and pepper. Transfer to a sauce-boat and serve hot with poultry or meat.

Makes about 250 ml (8 fl oz/1 cup).

PIQUANT SAUCE

1 large onion
60 g (2 oz) butter
3 tablespoons plain flour
250 ml (8 fl oz/1 cup) dry white wine
250 ml (8 fl oz/1 cup) red or white vinegar
Salt and pepper
2 dill pickles, diced
1 teaspoon finely chopped fresh tarragon
2 teaspoons finely chopped fresh parsley
1 teaspoon finely chopped fresh chervil
1 beef stock cube
60 ml (2 fl oz/¼ cup) water

Thinly slice the onion.

Turn onion to cut across slices; finely dice. In a heavy-based saucepan, melt butter, then add onion and cook over moderate heat until golden. Sprinkle in flour and cook, stirring, for 8 to 10 minutes until flour turns brown. Mix together wine and vinegar. Gradually add to flour mixture, stirring constantly to make a smooth, creamy brown sauce. Add salt and pepper and simmer 15 minutes.

Add pickles and herbs. Dissolve stock cube in water and add to sauce; stir through. Continue simmering for 10 minutes. Serve hot with roast pork, ham or use for re-heating leftover meats.

Makes about 375 ml (12 fl oz/1½ cups).

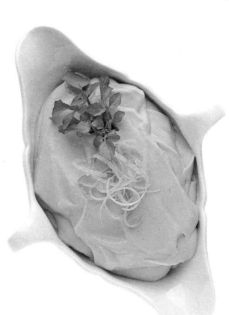

AVOCADO SAUCE

2 avocados
75 ml (2½ fl oz/⅓ cup) double (thickened)
   cream
75 ml (2½ fl oz/⅓ cup) water
½ teaspoon finely grated lemon rind
Juice of 1 lemon
Salt and pepper
4 teaspoons double (thickened) cream

Cut avocados in half; peel and remove
stones. Cut avocado flesh into pieces,
then place in a food processor fitted with
a metal blade. Add all ingredients,
except 4 teaspoons cream, then purée.

Transfer to a small heavy-based saucepan
over moderate heat and bring to the boil.
Lower heat and simmer gently until sauce
reduces to about 250 ml (8 fl oz/1 cup).
Remove from heat and cool slightly. Fold
in remaining cream.

Transfer to a sauce-boat and serve with
grilled Mediterranean (king) prawns,
chicken or poached salmon.

Makes about 250 ml (8 fl oz/1 cup).

SATAY SAUCE

30 g (1 oz) shredded unsweetened coconut
500 ml (16 fl oz/2 cups) boiling water
1 large onion, quartered
2 garlic cloves
6 small dried red chillies
1 tablespoon pine nuts
1 tablespoon finely grated lemon rind
2 tablespoons peanut oil
180 g (6 oz) crunchy peanut butter
1 teaspoon sugar
Salt

Place the coconut in a heatproof bowl and pour over boiling water. Stand about 30 minutes until cool. Squeeze through fine muslin to make coconut milk. Set milk aside; discard coconut.

Place onion, garlic, chillies, pine nuts and lemon rind in a food processor or blender and purée. Heat oil in a heavy-based saucepan and add the blended mixture. Cook over low heat for 3 to 4 minutes, stirring.

Add coconut milk to saucepan and bring to the boil, stirring constantly. Lower heat and add peanut butter, sugar and salt. Simmer for about 3 minutes. Serve hot over skewers of grilled marinated beef or chicken cubes. Cool, it makes a good dip for crudités.

Makes about 500 ml (16 fl oz/2 cups).

– BLUE CHEESE SAUCE & OYSTERS –

60 g (2 oz) butter
125 g (4 oz) blue cheese
1 large stalk celery, very finely chopped
1½ tablespoons Worcestershire sauce
75 ml (2½ fl oz/⅓ cup) soured cream
60 g (2 oz/½ cup) fresh white breadcrumbs
Pepper
1 egg, hard-boiled and chopped
24 oysters in the shells
Fresh dill sprigs or finely chopped fresh parsley

Melt butter in top of a double boiler over simmering water. Add cheese and celery. Cook 5 or 6 minutes, stirring frequently.

Add Worcestershire sauce, soured cream, breadcrumbs and pepper; combine well. Cool slightly. Stir in egg.

Heat oven to 190C (375F/Gas 5). Cover each oyster to top of shell with sauce. Place on baking trays and bake 8 to 10 minutes, until bubbling and lightly golden. Garnish with lemon wedges and dill sprigs. Serve hot.

Makes 24.

Note: If fresh oysters are unavailable, use canned oysters, well drained. Grill in ramekins or oyster shells.

—— CALIFORNIAN FISH SAUCE ——

60 g (2 oz) butter
30 g (1 oz/¼ cup) plain flour
Salt
45 g (1½ oz/¼ cup) light brown sugar
125 ml (4 fl oz/½ cup) water
Juice of 2 large lemons
60 g (2 oz/⅓ cup) seedless sultanas
Lemon slice

In a heavy-based saucepan melt butter, then stir in flour. Stir for about 3 minutes over low heat, without letting the flour brown. Add salt and brown sugar.

Warm water and lemon juice in a separate saucepan; stir into flour and butter. Whisk to blend well; cook over moderate heat for 5 to 6 minutes or until thick.

Add sultanas; continue cooking over low heat until sultanas are warm through. Pour into a warmed serving bowl; garnish with a lemon slice and serve with grilled white fish fillets.

Makes about 250 ml (8 fl oz/1 cup).

CREAMY CURRY SAUCE

2 tablespoons butter
2 medium onions, finely chopped
1 garlic clove
½ teaspoon grated fresh root ginger
1 tablespoon curry powder
500 ml (16 fl oz/2 cups) White Sauce, page 19

In a heavy-based saucepan, melt butter over low heat. Sauté onions, garlic and ginger; remove garlic clove after 1 or 2 minutes, because only a hint of its flavour is needed. Continue cooking over low heat until the onion is becoming soft and golden, but not brown.

Stir in curry powder. Cook a few minutes longer over low heat, taking care not to brown onions. Add White Sauce to onions and mix thoroughly. Serve hot, spooned over hot-boiled eggs, chicken or lamb.

Alternatively, increase butter to 60g (2 oz/¼ cup). Add 60g (2 oz/½ cup) plain flour with the curry powder; stir into the onions, ginger and butter. Cook about 3 minutes until bubbly. Stir in 500 ml (16 fl oz/2 cups) warm milk and bring to a boil. Serve hot, as above.

Makes about 500 ml (16 fl oz/2 cups).

— THAI GREEN CURRY SAUCE —

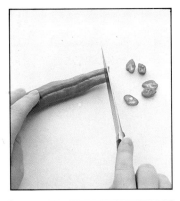

4 large, fresh green chillies
1 teaspoon black peppercorns
1 small onion, chopped
1 tablespoon chopped garlic
2 tablespoons chopped fresh coriander
2 teaspoons finely grated lemon rind
1 teaspoon salt
2 teaspoons ground coriander
1 teaspoon ground cumin
1 teaspoon ground cinnamon
2 teaspoons dried shrimp paste
1 teaspoon tumeric
1 tablespoon vegetable oil

Coarsely chop chillies, then seed.

Blend remaining ingredients to a paste, adding extra oil or water if needed.
Makes about 40 ml (2 fl oz/¼ cup).

GREEN FISH CURRY

600 ml (20 fl oz/2½ cups) coconut milk
2 tablespoons Thai Green Curry Paste, see above
500 g (1 lb) fish steaks, such as halibut
1 teaspoon salt
1 tablespoon soy sauce
1 teaspoon sesame oil
1 or 2 fresh green chillies
2 tablespoons finely chopped fresh basil

Combine coconut milk and curry paste; bring to the boil, stirring constantly. Add fish, salt, soy sauce and sesame oil; lower heat and simmer about 15 minutes until fish is cooked through and flakes easily. Add chillies and basil and simmer about 2 minutes.

Serves 4.

CURRIED CHICKEN SAUCE

3 tablespoons vegetable oil
750 g (1 ½ lb) cubed chicken breasts (fillets)
2 onions
2 cloves garlic
2 teaspoons grated fresh root ginger
½ teaspoon cayenne pepper
½ teaspoon turmeric
1 teaspoon curry powder
1 bay leaf
250 g (8 oz) tomatoes, skinned and chopped
½ teaspoon salt
2 tablespoons finely chopped fresh coriander or
   parsley
Hot water as needed

In a heavy-based frying pan, heat oil, add chicken and brown on all sides. Remove chicken and set aside.

Sauté onions, garlic and ginger until the onions are golden brown, stirring often. Add cayenne pepper, turmeric, curry powder and bay leaf and cook for 1 to 2 minutes.

Add tomatoes and salt; mix well. Return chicken to pan and simmer, half covered, over low heat for 30 minutes or until chicken is tender, stirring occasionally. Stir in coriander. If sauce is too thick, add a little hot water. Serve hot over boiled rice.

Makes 4 servings. .

PESTO SAUCE

30 g (1 oz/1¼ cups) fresh basil leaves, tightly
    packed
2 garlic cloves
Coarse or rock salt
2 tablespoons pine nuts
125 ml (4 fl oz/½ cup) olive oil
2 tablespoons freshly grated Parmesan cheese
2 tablespoons freshly grated pecorino cheese, or
    additional 2 tablespoons freshly grated
    Parmesan

Place basil, garlic, salt and pine nuts in a
blender or food processor. Whirl until
finely chopped.

With motor running, add oil in a thin
stream. Scrape down sides to make sure
all solids are well mixed. Continue
blending to make a smooth sauce.

Add cheeses and give the machine one
short burst to blend ingredients well.
Serve hot over freshly-cooked pasta.

Makes about 500 ml (16 fl oz/2 cups).

Note: Use only a high-quality olive oil
and do not substitute vegetable or peanut
oil. If the sauce is too thick, thin with a
little of the pasta cooking water. Store
any leftover sauce in a sealed container in
the refrigerator for up to 1 month.

MEXICAN-STYLE SAUCE

¾ lb. lean chuck steak
60 ml (2 fl oz/¼ cup) vegetable oil
2 small onions, finely chopped
1 garlic clove, finely chopped
315 ml (10 fl oz/1¼ cups) Tomato Sauce 2, page 21
315 ml (10 fl oz/1¼ cups) water
2 large tomatoes, peeled, seeded and chopped
1 teaspoon chilli powder
2 teaspoons ground cumin
60 g (2 oz/½ cup) grated Cheddar cheese plus extra for serving
2 tablespoons finely chopped, fresh parsley
½ teaspoon salt
½ teaspoon pepper
12 x 15 cm (6 in) corn tortillas, to serve
Melted butter
Shredded lettuce, to serve

Cut meat, across grain, into small pieces.

In a heavy-based saucepan heat oil; add onions and garlic and sauté until onions are light gold and soft. Add meat and cook over moderate heat until well browned. Mix the tomato sauce and water; add with remaining ingredients. Bring just to the boil; then lower heat and cook gently for 2 to 3 hours.

Brush tortillas with melted butter and warm in a 180C (350F/Gas 4) oven for 25 minutes. To serve, equally divide sauce between tortillas. Accompany with remaining grated cheese and shredded lettuce.

Makes about 600 ml (20 fl oz/2½ cups).

CARIBBEAN CREOLE SAUCE

125 ml (4 fl oz/½ cup) vegetable oil
2 medium onions, chopped
1 medium green pepper (capsicum), cored,
  seeded and finely chopped
2 garlic cloves
1 teaspoon finely chopped, seeded fresh red chilli
1 teaspoon salt
Pepper
3 tomatoes, skinned and chopped
180 g (6 oz) tomato purée (paste)
125 ml (4 fl oz/½ cup) dry white wine

In a heavy-based saucepan, heat oil over moderate heat. Add onions, green pepper (capsicum), garlic and chilli; sauté until the peppers are soft.

Add salt and pepper and tomatoes. Cook about 10 minutes over low heat, stirring occasionally.

Add tomato purée (paste) and wine and simmer, stirring occasionally. Serve the piquant sauce hot with boiled rice or grilled chicken.

Makes about 500 ml (16 fl oz/2 cups).

AMERICAN CREOLE SAUCE

4 medium mushrooms
60 g (2 oz) butter
1 medium onion
½ large green pepper (capsicum), cored, seeded
    and finely chopped
¼ red pepper (capsicum), cored, seeded and
    finely chopped
4 fresh parsley sprigs, finely chopped
500 ml (16 fl oz/2 cups) Sauce Espagnole, page
    16
Salt and pepper
Cayenne pepper

Finely slice mushrooms.

In a heavy-based saucepan, melt butter
over low heat. Add mushrooms, onion,
green and red peppers (capsicums) and
parsley. Cook 9 to 10 minutes until
peppers are soft.

In a separate saucepan, warm Sauce
Espagnole. Add to vegetables with
generous amounts of salt, pepper and
cayenne, according to taste. Bring just to
the boil; lower heat and simmer,
covered, 45 to 50 minutes. Transfer to a
sauce-boat and serve hot with grilled or
pan-fried steaks.

Makes about 500 ml (16 fl oz/2 cups).

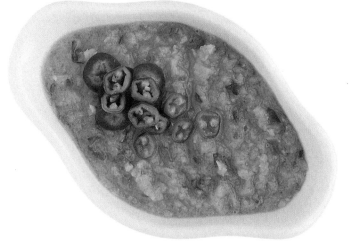

HOT FISH SAUCE

2 small fresh red chillies
60 ml (2 fl oz/¼ cup) olive oil
60 ml (2 fl oz/¼ cup) white wine vinegar
2 small onions, coarsely chopped
1 teaspoon lime or lemon juice
Salt and pepper

Cut chillies in half lengthways and remove seeds; finely chop.

Place all ingredients, except the chillies, in a blender or food processor and blend until the onions are puréed into the liquid. Add chillies to onion mixture and stir through.

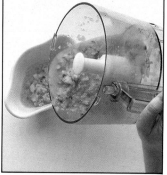

Transfer to a serving dish and let stand for 1 to 2 hours before serving. It will have developed its maximum zest by then.

Makes about 125 ml (4 fl oz/½ cup).

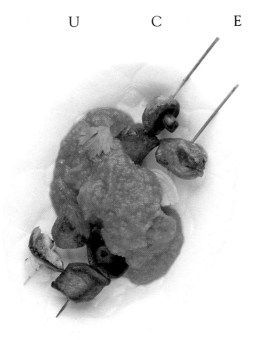

CHILLI SAUCE

10 garlic cloves
6 large onions, finely chopped
125 ml (4 fl oz/½ cup) vegetable oil
200 g (7 oz) fresh red chillies, seeded and
    chopped
375 g (12 oz/1½ cups) ketchup

Peel the garlic cloves, then finely chop.

In a heavy-based saucepan, gently fry onions in oil until they are soft; add the garlic and cook for 2 minutes. Add chillies and simmer for about 5 minutes.

Place the mixture in a food processor; add ketchup and purée. Return mixture to saucepan and simmer 15 minutes. Cool. This keeps for several months if closely covered and refrigerated. Place whatever you immediately don't use in hot sterilized screw-top jars or bottles and store for later use. Serve as a dipping sauce or incorporated into other sauces, such as pasta sauces.

Makes about 750 ml (24 fl oz/3 cups).

PORTUGUESE SAUCE

1 teaspoon olive oil
1 spring onion, finely chopped
1 garlic clove, crushed
4 large ripe tomatoes, peeled, seeded and chopped
Salt and pepper
2 tablespoons Sauce Espagnole, page 16, or
   Quick Brown Sauce, page 17
1 tablespoon tomato purée (paste)
Chopped fresh parsley, if desired

Heat oil in a small saucepan and sauté onion and garlic over low heat for 2-3 minutes, until soft but not coloured.

Add tomatoes, salt and pepper, and sauté until the tomatoes are soft. Add sauce and tomato purée (paste) and bring to a simmer for 1 to 2 minutes.

Add chopped parsley, if desired. Serve hot with meat or poultry.

Makes about 250 ml (8 fl oz/1 cup).

TOMATO COULIS

375 g (12 oz) ripe tomatoes
2 teaspoons vegetable oil
1 teaspoon lemon juice
1 small garlic clove
Salt and pepper

Boil enough water to cover the tomatoes. Pour boiling water over tomatoes and let stand for 15 seconds only. Run them under cold water, then skin. Chop and purée in a blender or food processor, then pass through a strainer. Place in a bowl. Stir in oil and lemon juice.

Squeeze garlic through a garlic press into the tomato mixture.

Add salt and pepper. Stir thoroughly to combine all ingredients. Cover and refrigerate until ready to use. Serve chilled with hot or cold meat.

Makes about 250 ml (8 fl oz/1 cup).

SAUCE MOUSSELINE

125 ml (4 fl oz/½ cup) double (thickened) cream
250 ml (8 fl oz/1 cup) Hollandaise Sauce, page
  22, kept warm
2 eggs, hard-boiled, shelled and cut in half

Whip cream until stiff.

In top of double boiler over simmering water fold cream into Hollandaise Sauce; gently fold until well blended. Transfer to serving dish.

Serve hot over hard-boiled eggs, or lightly-cooked fresh vegetables, such as green beans, asparagus or artichokes. The sauce also goes well with poached salmon.

Makes about 375 ml (12 fl oz/1½ cups).

PARSLEY SAUCE

15 g (½ oz/¾ cup) chopped fresh parsley
½ teaspoon lemon juice
1 whole nutmeg
250 ml (8 fl oz/1 cup) Béchamel Sauce, page 18,
    kept hot

Place half the parsley in a small heatproof bowl and add just enough boiling water to cover. Let stand for 5 minutes, then strain, reserving the liquid.

Place the lemon juice in a small bowl. Grate in nutmeg to taste. Add reserved parsley liquid and stir well.

Pour into hot Béchamel Sauce and mix through. Add remaining parsley. Serve hot with seafood or vegetables, such as cauliflower or steamed carrots.

Makes about 250 ml (8 fl oz/1 cup).

CHEESE SAUCE

90 g (3 oz) Cheddar Cheese
2 tablespoons butter
2 tablespoons plain flour
125 ml (4 fl oz/½ cup) milk
125 ml (4 fl oz/½ cup) additional milk or
　　vegetable cooking water
½ teaspoon prepared mustard
1 chicken stock cube, crumbled
3 or 4 drops Tabasco sauce
60 ml (2 fl oz/¼ cup) dry sherry

Grate cheese and set aside. In a small
heavy-based saucepan, melt butter. Add
flour, and stir continuously over
moderate heat until bubbly. Combine
milk with vegetable water, if using.
Using a whisk gradually pour into
saucepan.

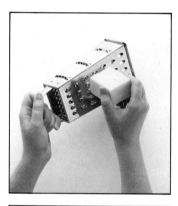

Use a wire whisk to combine into a
creamy sauce. Add remaining
ingredients except the cheese and stir
gently until sauce boils and thickens.

Add cheese and stir until melted
through. Transfer to a sauce-boat and
serve hot over lightly cooked vegetables,
chicken or fish.

Makes about 375 ml (12 fl oz/1½ cups).

BOLOGNAISE SAUCE

60 g (2 oz) butter
1 medium onion, finely chopped
1 celery stalk, finely chopped
1 small carrot, finely chopped
125 g (4 oz) bacon rashers, including fat, finely
    chopped
250 g (8 oz) minced beef
Salt and pepper
Pinch of ground nutmeg
1 tablespoon finely chopped fresh oregano, or ½
    teaspoon dried oregano
125 ml (4 fl oz/½ cup) dry white wine
250 ml (8 fl oz/1 cup) beef stock or 1 beef stock
    cube dissolved in boiling water
2 tablespoons tomato purée (paste)
2 chicken livers, if desired, finely chopped
125 ml (4 fl oz/½ cup) double (thickened) cream

Melt butter in a large, heavy-based saucepan. Add onion, celery, carrot and bacon. Cook over moderate heat until the onion is golden and soft.

Add beef and cook until is no longer pink, stirring often to prevent sticking. Add salt, pepper, nutmeg and oregano. Increase heat to high and pour in wine. Bring to the boil, stirring constantly, and cook until the wine has almost evaporated. Add beef stock and tomato purée (paste) and simmer for 35 to 40 minutes, uncovered, stirring often.

A few minutes before serving, add the chicken livers, if desired. Add cream and stir. Serve hot with pasta.

Makes about 600 ml (20 fl oz/2½ cups).

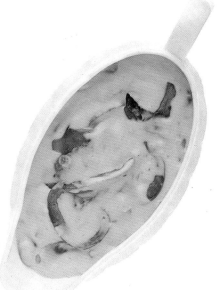

À La King Sauce

60 g (2 oz) butter
¼ green pepper (capsicum), cored, seeded and cut in short thin strips
¼ red pepper (capsicum), cored, seeded and cut in short thin strips
125 g (4 oz) mushrooms, thinly sliced
60 g (2 oz/½ cup) plain flour
Salt
¼ teaspoon white pepper
500 ml (16 fl oz/2 cups) milk
1 egg yolk, lightly beaten
2 tablespoons dry sherry, if desired

In a large, heavy based saucepan, melt the butter over moderate heat. Add green and red pepper (capsicum) strips and sauté for 1 to 2 minutes.

Add the mushrooms and sauté over low heat until the peppers are soft. Add the flour, salt and pepper and blend. Warm milk and pour into saucepan all at once, using a whisk to produce a smooth sauce.

Bring sauce to the boil. Stir a little of the hot sauce into the egg yolk. Lower the heat to low and stir in egg yolk. Add sherry, if desired. Serve sauce hot poured over chicken breasts (fillets) or with chunks of hot cooked chicken for a light dish.

Makes about 600 ml (1 pint/2½ cups).

BREAD SAUCE

6 whole cloves
500 ml (16 fl oz/2 cups) milk
1 medium onion
Pinch of ground mace
2 tablespoons butter
2 tablespoons double (thickened) cream, or use
   extra butter
Salt and white pepper
Pinch of cayenne pepper
60 g (2 oz/1 cup) fresh white breadcrumbs, no
   crusts

Stick cloves in onion. Place milk and mace in a heavy-based saucepan.

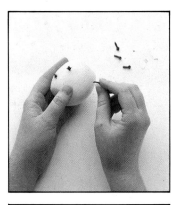

Add onion and bring to the boil. Simmer 15 minutes or more to flavour milk thoroughly. Remove onion and any loose cloves with a slotted spoon.

Add butter, cream, seasonings and breadcrumbs. Stir constantly over low heat until the sauce thickens. Serve hot with roast beef or poultry.

Makes about 500 ml (16 fl oz/2 cups).

PAPRIKA SAUCE

½ tablespoon butter
1 tablespoon finely chopped onion
1 tablespoon paprika, plus extra for sprinkling
250 ml (8 fl oz/1 cup) Béchamel Sauce, page 18,
　　or White Sauce, page 19
60 ml (2 fl oz/¼ cup) double (thickened) cream

In a small saucepan, melt butter over low heat. Sauté onion and paprika until onion is soft and golden.

In a separate saucepan, simmer Béchamel Sauce, stirring often, for 1 to 2 minutes. Add cooked onion and paprika.

Add cream, stirring constantly until heated through. Transfer to a serving dish, sprinkle with extra paprika, if desired, and serve hot with chicken, fish and veal.

Makes about 250 ml (8 fl oz/1 cup).

WALNUT SAUCE

30 g (1 oz/¼ cup) plain flour
180 ml (6 fl oz/¾ cup) freshly-squeezed orange
 juice
1 tablespoon lemon juice
1 chicken stock cube, dissolved in 125 ml
 (4 fl oz/½ cup) boiling water
1 tablespoon finely shredded orange rind
60 g (2 oz) walnuts, chopped

Prepare this sauce in a frying pan that
chicken breasts (fillets) have just been
cooked in; remove breasts and keep hot.
Sprinkle flour into the hot frying pan.
Stir over moderate heat for 3 minutes to
cook the flour without letting it brown.

Slowly add the orange and lemon juices,
mixed together, stirring vigorously to
avoid lumps. Add chicken stock all at
once, then stir over low heat until the
sauce is smooth and thickened.

Stir in orange rind and walnuts. Cook for
1 to 2 minutes and serve with the
chicken.

Makes about 375 ml (12 fl oz/1½ cups).

Note: If not cooking chicken breasts,
melt 3 tablespoons butter in the pan.

CELERY SAUCE

2 to 3 celery stalks
500 ml (16 fl oz/2 cups) White Stock, page 9, or 2
   chicken stock cubes, dissolved in 500 ml (16 fl
   oz/2 cups) boiling water
60 g (2 oz) butter
30 g (1 oz/¼ cup) plain flour
125 ml (4 fl oz/½ cup) double (thickened) cream
Salt
½ teaspoon white pepper

Finely chop celery stalks and leaves.

In a saucepan over moderate heat, add celery and stock. Cook 10 to 12 minutes or until celery is tender and soft. Drain celery and reserve cooking liquid; keep hot. In a heavy-based saucepan, melt butter, add flour and cook over low heat, stirring constantly, until bubbly. Do not let flour brown. Gradually whisk in hot celery cooking liquid.

Continue whisking until the mixture comes to the boil. Lower heat, add celery and simmer 10 minutes. Purée in a blender or food processor, then rub through fine strainer to remove strings. Return to saucepan and warm through. Add cream, salt and pepper. Serve hot with smoked mackerel fillets, chicken, rabbit or lamb.

Makes about 750 ml (24 fl oz/3 cups).

TARTARE SAUCE

1 tablespoon capers, drained
1 tablespoon finely chopped dill pickles
1 tablespoon finely chopped fresh parsley
250 ml (8 fl oz/1 cup) Mayonnaise, page 14
1 teaspoon lemon juice
Salt and pepper

Finely chop the capers.

In a bowl, stir the capers, pickles and parsley into the Mayonnaise.

Stir in lemon juice. Adjust the flavour if necessary, with salt and pepper, or more lemon juice. Serve cold with grilled or fried fish.

Makes about 315 ml (10 fl oz/1¼ cups).

Note: Store for up to 1 week in a well-sealed container in the refrigerator; add 1 tablespoon boiling water before sealing.

MUSHROOM SAUCE

180 g (6 oz) mushrooms
3 tablespoons butter
500 ml (16 fl oz/2 cups) Béchamel Sauce, page
  18, kept warm
Salt and pepper
Paprika, if desired

Remove the stalks from mushrooms and reserve for other uses. Wash the caps and dry on absorbent kitchen paper.

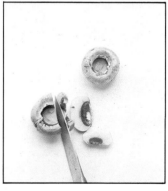

Finely slice mushroom caps.

In a frying pan over low heat, melt butter, sauté mushrooms until lightly browned. Add mushrooms to the just-cooked Béchamel Sauce. Season to taste with salt and pepper. Transfer to a sauce-boat and sprinkle with paprika. Serve hot with chicken or fish.

Makes about 500 ml (16 fl oz/2 cups).

EGG SAUCE

2 eggs, hard-boiled
1 tablespoon parsley without stems, finely
   chopped
1 teaspoon lemon juice
375 ml (12 fl oz/1½ cups) Béchamel Sauce, page
   18, kept hot

Remove yolks from hard-boiled eggs and rub through a coarse strainer.

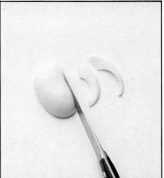

Cut whites into thin, short strips. Combine yolks and whites, then add parsley. Set aside.

In a heavy-based saucepan over moderate heat, add lemon juice to the hot Béchamel Sauce, stirring to prevent it curdling. Add egg and parsley mixture. Serve hot with steamed or poached fish.

Makes about 375 ml (12 fl oz/1½ cups).

PEPPER SAUCE

60 g (2 oz) butter
½ large or 1 small carrot, chopped
1 medium onion, chopped
1 celery stalk, chopped
Bouquet garni (1 bay leaf, 1 fresh thyme sprig,
　4 fresh parsley sprigs, tied together, page 8)
2 teaspoons plain flour
180 ml (6 fl oz/¾ cup) red wine
1 tablespoon red wine vinegar
Add about ¼ teaspoon freshly ground pepper

In a small, heavy-based saucepan, melt butter, then add chopped vegetables and bouquet garni. Sauté, stirring often, until vegetables are beginning to brown. Add flour all at once and stir in with a wooden spoon. Cook over low heat until flour browns, stirring constantly.

Meanwhile, warm wine and vinegar in a small saucepan. Pour all at once into flour mixture. Blend thoroughly. Bring just to the boil and simmer gently, uncovered, for 20 minutes. Add pepper to taste and cook for 1 minute.

Pour through a fine strainer and serve hot with beef or venison or other game.

Makes about 250 ml (8 fl oz/1 cup).

SAUCE BERÇY

½ tablespoon butter
1 spring onion, finely chopped
125 ml (4 fl oz/½ cup) dry white wine
125 ml (4 fl oz/½ cup) Fish Velouté Sauce, page 12
2 teaspoons finely chopped fresh parsley

In a small, heavy-based saucepan, melt butter. Sauté spring onion in butter until soft but not browned.

Add wine and simmer over moderate heat until the liquid is reduced by half.

Add Fish Velouté Sauce and bring to a simmer, stirring often. Mix in parsley and serve hot with fried or poached fish fillets.

Makes about 180 ml (6 fl oz/¾ cup).

Note: To make a sauce to serve with veal, reduce Veal Velouté Sauce, page 12, by one-third and substitute for the Fish Velouté Sauce.

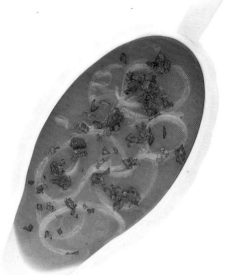

SAUCE LYONNAISE

125 g (4 oz) butter
2 onions, finely chopped
180 ml (6 fl oz/¾ cup) dry white wine
180 ml (6 fl oz/¾ cup) white wine vinegar
250 ml (8 fl oz/1 cup) Sauce Espagnole, page 16
2 tablespoons butter
1 small onion, thinly sliced
Finely chopped fresh parsley

In a heavy-based saucepan, melt butter. Sauté onions over low heat until they are soft and golden brown.

Add wine and vinegar and simmer until reduced to about 250 ml (8 fl oz/1 cup). Add Sauce Espagnole and cook gently for about 10 minutes, stirring constantly.

Meanwhile, melt remaining butter in a frying pan and sauté onion rings until they are tender. Add to sauce immediately before serving. Transfer to a sauce-boat, sprinkle with parsley and serve hot with pork or lightly cooked vegetables or with leftover meat.

Makes about 500 ml (16 fl oz/2 cups).

SAUCE POULETTE

1 tablespoon butter
4 small mushrooms, finely sliced
1 teaspoon grated onion
75 ml (2½ fl oz/⅓ cup) dry white wine
75 ml (2½ fl oz/⅓ cup) double (thickened) cream
180 ml (6 fl oz/¾ cup) Chicken Velouté Sauce, page 12
3 egg yolks
About 2 tablespoons lemon juice
1 tablespoon finely chopped fresh parsley

Using the top half of a double boiler over medium direct heat, melt butter and sauté mushrooms until they soften. Add the onion and wine and cook until wine has almost evaporated.

Lower the heat, stir in half the cream and cook for 5 minutes or until sauce has reduced by about half. Add the Velouté Sauce and bring to the boil.

Meanwhile, in a bowl lightly beat egg yolks into remaining cream; stir in a little of the hot sauce. With water briskly simmering in bottom half of double boiler, place on top half. Stir in egg and cream mixture. Cook, stirring, until very hot but not boiling. Add lemon juice and parsley. Serve hot with cooked jumbo Mediterranean (king) prawns or other shellfish.

Makes about 315 ml (10 fl oz/1¼ cups).

COCKTAIL SAUCE

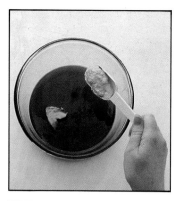

250 ml (8 fl oz/1 cup) ketchup
1 tablespoon Worcestershire sauce
1 tablespoon grated fresh horseradish
1 teaspoon cider vinegar
1 teaspoon prepared mustard
Juice of 1 lemon
Pinch of celery salt
3 or 4 drops Tabasco sauce
2 tablespoons double (thickened) cream
Selection prepared seafood, such as cooked
    prawns, to serve

In a medium bowl, thoroughly mix all the
ingredients, except Tabasco sauce and
cream, using a fork to lightly whisk.

Add Tabasco sauce to taste.

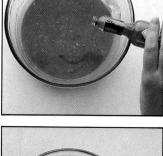

Stir in cream. Cover and store in the
refrigerator for up to 2 days. Serve chilled
with the prepared seafood of your choice.

Makes about 250 ml (8 fl oz/1 cup).

CAPER SAUCE

500 ml (16 fl oz/2 cups) White Sauce, page 19,
   using 250 ml (8 fl oz/1 cup) milk and water in
   which ham has been boiled in instead of 500 ml
   (16 fl oz/2 cups) milk
75 ml (2½ fl oz/⅓ cup) double (thickened)
   cream
3 tablespoons bottled capers, with 2 teaspoons
   pickling liquid reserved

When White Sauce is ready, stir in
cream.

Quickly add the capers and their liquid.
Mix thoroughly and it is ready to serve
with lamb or ham. Do not cook any
further, or the capers and pickling liquid
may curdle the sauce.

If not serving at once, cover closely with
cling film to prevent skin forming.
Re-heat gently in top of double boiler.

Makes about 600 ml (20 fl oz/2½ cups).

Note: 2 teaspoons lemon juice can be
substituted for the caper pickling liquid.

CHÂTELAINE SAUCE

2 medium onions, finely chopped
4 large mushrooms, chopped
1 medium tomato, skinned, seeded and chopped
250 ml (8 fl oz/1 cup) dry white wine
Salt and pepper
250 ml (8 fl oz/1 cup) double (thickened) cream
1 bay leaf
6 fresh parsley sprigs

Make sauce in roasting pan that has just been used for roasting chicken, duck or turkey; remove poultry and keep hot. Keep 2 or 3 tablespoons of dripping in the pan. In a small saucepan, cook onions, mushrooms and tomato in the white wine with salt and pepper. Simmer until the liquid is reduced to about 2 tablespoons or less.

Pour mixture into roasting pan; stir thoroughly 2 to 3 minutes, over low heat. Set aside.

In another small saucepan, combine cream, bay leaf and parsley and cook over low heat, stirring constantly, until bubbly. Add to contents of the roasting pan. Stir well and bring to a boil. Strain, then serve hot with sliced poultry.

Makes about 250 ml (8 fl oz/1 cup).

SAUCE SUPRÊME

250 ml (8 fl oz/1 cup) chicken stock or water
45 g (1½ oz) mushrooms stalks and pieces
375 ml (12 fl oz/1½ cups) Chicken Velouté
    Sauce, page 12
180 ml (6 fl oz/¾ cup) double (thickened) cream

In a heavy-based saucepan, add stock and mushrooms. Bring to the boil and boil until liquid is reduced to about 125 ml (4 fl oz/½ cup). Remove from heat and keep hot.

In a separate small heavy-based saucepan, heat Chicken Velouté Sauce, bring to the boil. Lower heat and simmer about 10 minutes until reduced to 250 ml (8 fl oz/1 cup). Strain mushrooms and their liquid over sauce, discard mushrooms. Stir mushroom-flavoured stock into sauce.

Slowly add cream, stirring constantly. When cream is heated through, serve hot with roast chicken, poached fish or over hard-boiled eggs.

Makes about 500 ml (16 fl oz/2 cups).

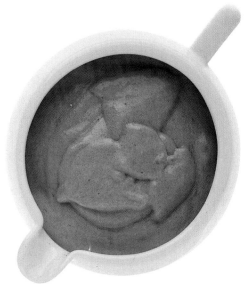

SAUCE CHORON

4 tablespoons dry white wine
4 tablespoons white wine vinegar
1 spring onion, finely chopped
3 egg yolks
180 g (6 oz) to 250 g (8 oz) butter, cut into pieces
Salt and white pepper
125 g (4 oz/½ cup) tomato purée (paste),
    reduced by boiling to 60 g (2 oz/¼ cup)

In a small saucepan, combine wine and vinegar, then add spring onion and cook over low heat until the liquid is reduced by half. Set aside to cool.

Strain and put liquid in the top of a double boiler over simmering water. Whisk the egg yolks in until light and fluffy. Add butter, one piece at a time, stirring thoroughly after each addition. The sauce should be like a smooth mayonnaise but you may need extra butter to achieve the correct consistency.

Add the tomato purée (paste). Heat mixture until warm, place in a serving bowl and serve with grilled meat, fish and chicken.

Makes about 315 ml (10 fl oz/1¼ cups).

NEWBURG SAUCE

2 tablespoons butter
250 ml (8 fl oz/1 cup) double (thickened) cream
5 tablespoons dry sherry or Madeira
½ teaspoon salt
Pinch of cayenne pepper
3 egg yolks, well beaten
Lobster coral, if available

In the top half of a double boiler over very low direct heat, melt butter and add cream. When cream is hot but not boiling, stir in 4 tablespoons sherry and season with salt and cayenne pepper. Bring almost to the boil.

Place over simmering water in the lower half of the double boiler.

Stir in the egg yolks and whisk until the sauce has thickened and is smooth. If serving with lobster, add coral for extra flavour. Add remaining 1 tablespoon sherry immediately before serving. Serve hot at once with lobster, Mediterranean (king) prawns, scallops or freshly cooked vegetables, such as cauliflower, broccoli or asparagus.

Makes 375 ml (12 fl oz/1½ cups).

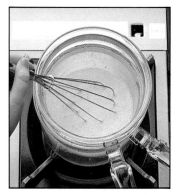

CRAB SAUCE

125 g (4 oz) crab meat, fresh or canned
1 teaspoon prepared mustard
4 tablespoons tarragon vinegar
1 small bunch fresh chives
250 ml (8 fl oz/1 cup) White Sauce, page 19

Flake crab meat, removing all cartilage, then set aside.

In a bowl, combine the mustard and vinegar. Snip in 2 teaspoons chives then add the flaked crab meat. Marinate for about 15 minutes.

Carefully squeeze out the vinegar and discard. In a small saucepan, warm White Sauce, then add crab meat mixture. Cook for a few minutes to gently heat the crab meat. Serve warm with grilled or steamed fish.

Makes 375 ml (12 fl oz/1½ cups).

VARIATION:
By doubling the quantity of crab meat, you can prepare a simple and delicious first course. Place the thick Crab Sauce in scallop shells and decorated with extra snipped chives and lemon twists.

SAUCE MATELOTE

1 garlic clove
2 tablespoons butter
125 ml (4 fl oz/½ cup) Fish Stock, page 10
750 ml (24 fl oz/3 cups) red or white wine
1½ tablespoons plain flour
Extra butter
Cayenne pepper for sprinkling

Crush the garlic by bruising it with the side of a knife.

In a heavy-based saucepan, melt 1 tablespoon of the butter and gently fry the garlic until golden. Remove garlic and add Fish Stock. Bring to the boil and reduce sauce to about half. Pour in wine and continue cooking over moderate heat until the liquid has reduced to about 375 ml (12 fl oz/1½ cups).

Meanwhile, make a beurre manié by combining remaining 1 tablespoon butter with flour. Add beurre manié, a little at a time, stirring constantly. Bring to the boil. Float a little extra butter on top. Sprinkle with cayenne pepper and serve hot with poached fish.

Makes about 375 ml (12 fl oz/1½ cups).

MARINARA SAUCE

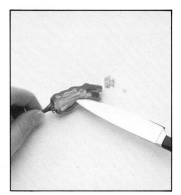

1 to 2 small fresh red chillies, according to taste
12 large black olives, stoned and chopped
1 tablespoon capers, drained
125 ml (4 fl oz/½ cup) olive oil
1 medium onion, finely chopped
2 garlic cloves, finely chopped
2 teaspoons chopped fresh oregano or
   ½ teaspoon dried oregano
500 g (1 lb) ripe tomatoes or 500 g (1 lb) canned
   skinned tomatoes

Slice each chilli and use the tip of a knife to remove seeds.

In a glass or ceramic bowl, marinate the olives, chillies and capers in 4 tablespoons oil for at least 1 hour. Meanwhile, gently sauté the onion and garlic in the remaining oil until golden. Add the oregano.

Skin fresh tomatoes; use a spoon to scoop out seeds, then chop. Strain canned tomatoes. Turn all ingredients into a flameproof casserole or large frying pan and cook over moderate to high heat until the mixture thickens and darkens slightly. Remove chillies. Serve the sauce hot with pasta.

Makes about 500 ml (16 fl oz/2 cups).

LEMON-MUSTARD SAUCE

90 g (3 oz) butter
45 g (1½ oz/3 tablespoons) plain flour
375 ml (12 fl oz/1½ cups) chicken or beef stock,
   or White Stock, page 9
3 egg yolks
2 tablespoons lemon juice
2 teaspoons Dijon mustard
Salt
Cayenne pepper

In a heavy-based medium saucepan, melt butter and add the flour all at once. Cook, stirring constantly, for 3 minutes.

Add stock all at once, whisking to blend smoothly. Cook over low heat, stirring often, for 5 to 6 minutes.

Remove from heat and gently beat in egg yolks and add lemon juice, whisking constantly. Add mustard and mix well, then add salt. Return to heat and cook 1 to 2 minutes longer, then add cayenne pepper, a little at a time, stirring and tasting until required degree of heat is achieved. Serve hot over steamed or boiled vegetables, such as asparagus, or use as an accompaniment for fish.

Makes about 500 ml (16 fl oz/2 cups).

MUSTARD SAUCE

250 ml (8 fl oz/1 cup) Béchamel Sauce, page 18,
   kept hot
60 ml (2 fl oz/¼ cup) double (thickened) cream
½ lemon
1 teaspoon prepared mustard
1 teaspoon Dijon mustard
Fresh herb sprigs, to garnish

In a heavy-based saucepan, combine
Béchamel Sauce and cream. Squeeze in
the juice from the lemon, removing seeds.

Stir in the mustards.

Serve hot, garnished with fresh herb
sprigs, over grilled or poached fish or
steamed green vegetables.

Makes about 315 ml (10 fl oz/1¼ cups).

MINT SAUCE

1½ to 2 tablespoons caster sugar, or to taste
2 tablespoons young, fresh mint leaves, washed
   and dried
1 tablespoon boiling water
125 ml (4 fl oz/½ cup) red wine vinegar or malt
   vinegar

To bring out mint flavour, sprinkle sugar over mint leaves.

Finely chop mint sprigs. Scrape mint and sugar into a bowl, then add boiling water and stir until the sugar is dissolved.

Allow to cool a little, add the vinegar, cover and refrigerate. Serve cold with lamb.

Makes about 125 ml (4 fl oz/½ cup).

IVORY SAUCE

40 g (2 oz) mushrooms, chopped
White pepper
About 250 ml (8 fl oz/1 cup) water
500 ml (16 fl oz/2 cups) chicken or fish stock
60 g (2 oz) butter
30 g (1 oz/¼ cup) plain flour
2 eggs
Salt and pepper
Chopped fresh tarragon, if desired

In a medium saucepan, add mushrooms, pepper and enough water to cover. Cook over a moderate heat until the mushrooms are soft. Strain off water and add to chicken or fish stock. Discard mushrooms. In a medium saucepan, boil this liquid over moderate heat until reduced to about 500 ml (16 fl oz/2 cups).

In a heavy-based saucepan, melt butter, stir in flour and cook, stirring constantly, for 3 minutes. Add stock while still hot, then continue to stir until sauce comes to the boil. Simmer for about 5 minutes, stirring often. The sauce should be quite creamy; if it thickens too much, add a little extra stock or water.

Beat eggs with 1 teaspoon hot stock. Remove sauce from heat and whisk in eggs until all frothiness has been absorbed into sauce. You should have a velvety textured, creamy sauce. Add salt and pepper to taste. Sprinkle with finely chopped fresh tarragon and serve hot with poached chicken or fish.

Makes about 500 ml (16 fl oz/2 cups).

MADEIRA SAUCE

75 ml (2½ fl oz/⅓ cup) Madeira
375 ml (12 fl oz/1½ cups) Sauce Espagnole,
   page 16
2 tablespoons butter

This sauce is best served with sautéed beef fillets, chicken breasts or veal; remove the meat or poultry from the frying pan and keep hot. Add all but 1 tablespoon Madeira to the pan. Heat over low heat and stir with a wooden spoon to combine the wine with juices.

Meanwhile, in a small saucepan, simmer Sauce Espagnole over low heat until reduced to a little over 250 ml (8 fl oz/1 cup). Add to pan and stir well while heating through.

Melt in butter. Add remaining 1 tablespoon Madeira immediately before serving. Serve hot with the cooked meat or chicken.

Makes about 250 ml (8 fl oz/1 cup).

Note: Dry sherry can be substituted for the Madeira.

CUCUMBER SAUCE

250 ml (8 fl oz/1 cup) milk
1 onion slice
1 whole clove
½ bay leaf
1 sprig fresh parsley
60 g (2 oz) butter
30 g (1 oz/¼ cup) plain flour
Salt and pepper
1 egg yolk, beaten
½ cucumber, quartered and sliced
½ teaspoon chopped fresh chervil
1 teaspoon snipped fresh chives

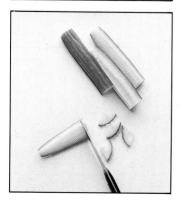

In a medium saucepan, warm milk, add onion, clove and herbs. In another saucepan, melt butter, then stir in flour until well blended. Cook over low heat for 3 minutes, stirring occasionally. Season lightly with salt and pepper.

Remove onion, clove and herbs from milk. Add flavoured milk all at once into flour mixture, whisking to make a smooth sauce. Stir continually over low heat until the sauce just begins to bubble and become thick. Remove from heat. Mix a little of the hot sauce with the egg yolk, then quickly whisk in the egg yolk.

Finely chop the cucumber. Add to the sauce with the chervil and chives. Cook for 1 to 2 minutes, without boiling. Pour into a sauce-boat and serve hot with seafood, such as poached salmon.

Makes about 375 ml (12 fl oz/1½ cups).

GRIBICHE SAUCE

3 eggs, hard-boiled
½ teaspoon Dijon mustard
½ teaspoon prepared mustard
Salt
About 250 ml (8 fl oz/1 cup) olive oil
4 tablespoons vinegar
1 garlic clove, crushed
2 gherkins, finely chopped
1 teaspoon finely chopped fresh tarragon
1 teaspoon finely chopped fresh chervil
1 teaspoon finely snipped fresh chives
2 teaspoons finely chopped fresh parsley
8 capers, drained and chopped

Separate egg yolks from whites. Cut whites in small thin strips and set aside. Place 3 egg yolks in a bowl and mash to a paste. Add mustards and salt and mix thoroughly.

Whisk in oil, a little at a time. As mixture begins to thicken, increase oil to a slow stream, and start adding vinegar, beating constantly. Use only the amount of oil required to reach a velvety consistency, not quite as thick as mayonnaise.

Add garlic, gherkins, herbs, capers and egg whites. Stir to mix through. Serve with cold fish, shellfish or meat.

Makes about 375 ml (12 fl oz/1½ cups).

HORSERADISH SAUCE

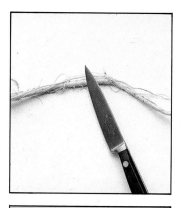

1 piece fresh horseradish, scrubbed
2 tablespoons caster sugar
Salt
½ teaspoon dry mustard
2 tablespoons milk
60 g (2 oz/½ cup) fresh white breadcrumbs
180 ml (6 fl oz/¾ cup) double (thickened) cream
1 tablespoon red wine vinegar

Cut any discoloured pieces from the horseradish, then cut away the outer part and finely grate; you should have 3 to 4 tablespoons.

Combine horseradish with sugar, salt and mustard in a bowl. In another small bowl, pour milk over breadcrumbs. Mix well. Squeeze out milk, leaving crumbs moist. Add crumbs to bowl with horseradish. Stir in cream and blend thoroughly.

Stir in vinegar. Cover and refrigerate until ready to serve. The sauce will keep in a screw-top jar for up to 1 week. Serve cold with hot roast beef.

Makes about 250 ml (8 fl oz/1 cup).

ONION SAUCE

2 medium to large onions
500 ml (16 fl oz/2 cups) milk
½ teaspoon grated nutmeg
Salt and pepper
1 bay leaf
60 g (2 oz) butter
60 g (2 oz/½ cup) plain flour

Cut the onions into eighths.

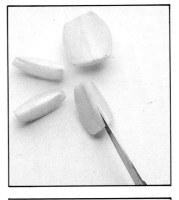

In a heavy-based saucepan over medium heat, cook onions in milk, seasoned with nutmeg, salt, pepper and bay leaf. Cook until onions are soft. Remove bay leaf.

Meanwhile, melt butter in a medium saucepan; add flour, stirring for 3 minutes or until bubbly. Add flavoured milk all at once and whisk until smooth. Cook over medium heat, stirring often, until just boiling; reduce heat and simmer for 5 to 7 minutes. If desired, strain, return to saucepan to heat through. Serve hot with steaks, rabbit, boiled lamb and corned beef.

Makes about 500 ml (16 fl oz/2 cups).

OLIVE SAUCE

20 black olives
60 g (2 oz) butter
30 g (1 oz/¼ cup) plain flour
125 ml (4 fl oz/½ cup) Fish Stock, page 10
125 ml (4 fl oz/½ cup) milk
1 tablespoon finely chopped fresh parsley
½ teaspoon finely chopped fresh oregano, or
 ¼ teaspoon dried oregano

Stone the olives, then cut olive flesh in thin strips.

Melt butter in a small saucepan and stir in flour. Cook over low heat for about 3 minutes, stirring continually, until bubbly. Warm Fish Stock with milk in a separate saucepan. Add milk-stock liquid all at once; whisk to a smooth sauce. Continue whisking gently until the sauce thickens. Simmer, stirring often, for 10 minutes.

Add olives, parsley and oregano and heat through well. Transfer to a sauce-boat and serve with steamed or poached seafood.

Makes about 250 ml (8 fl oz/1 cup).

Note: By substituting Sauce Espagnole, page 16, for the fish stock and milk used above, you will have a rich accompaniment for lamb.

SAUCE NANTUA

250 ml (8 fl oz/1 cup) Béchamel sauce, page 18
60 ml (2 fl oz/¼ cup) double (thickened) cream, scalded
2 tablespoons Lobster Butter, see below
Extra cooked lobster meat, shredded
LOBSTER BUTTER
1 to 2 lobster shells
1 tablespoon lobster meat
Lobster coral
2 tablespoons butter
2 tablespoons water

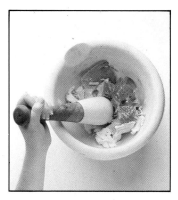

Begin by making the Lobster Butter; use a pestle and mortar to crush the shells, meat and coral with butter until shells are almost powdered.

Add lobster mixture to top of double boiler over simmering water with 2 tablespoons water. Cook for 20 minutes, stirring occasionally. Pass through a fine strainer into a small bowl, cover with cling film and refrigerate until firm; the butter rises to the surface and solidifies. Store butter until ready to use.

To make the sauce, heat Béchamel Sauce in top of double boiler over simmering water, then fold in cream. Meanwhile, melt Lobster Butter over low heat and add to sauce with extra lobster meat. Serve hot with boiled lobster or other seafood.

Makes about 250 ml (8 fl oz/1 cup).

BARBECUE SAUCE

125 g (4 oz) butter
1 medium onion, very finely chopped
1 garlic clove, crushed
250 ml (8 fl oz/1 cup) water
60 ml (2 fl oz/¼ cup) dry red wine
1 teaspoon brown sugar
1 teaspoon salt
½ teaspoon freshly ground pepper
½ teaspoon chilli powder
4 drops Tabasco sauce
2 tablespoons Worcestershire sauce
2 tablespoons tomato ketchup

In a medium saucepan, melt butter over low heat. Add onion and garlic and cook until soft, but not brown.

Add all remaining ingredients and stir well. Bring to the boil, lower heat and simmer for about 15 minutes.

When cooled, refrigerate in a sealed jar for 2 to 3 weeks. As a sauce, it may be served cold, or reheated and served hot. Use with beef, but it is also delicious with barbecued chicken and lamb. To use as a marinade, place the meat in the liquid, cover, and refrigerate for 2 hours or more, turning the meat several times. Brush the marinade left in the dish over the meat as it cooks.

Makes about 315 ml (10 fl oz/1¼ cups).

CHARCUTERIE SAUCE

2 tablespoons butter
1 small onion, finely chopped
375 ml (12 fl oz/1½ cups) Sauce Espagnole, page 16
125 ml (4 fl oz/½ cup) dry white wine
2 dill pickles, cut in julienne strips

In a heavy-based saucepan, melt butter and sauté onion over moderate heat until soft and golden, but not brown.

Stir in Sauce Espagnole and wine, then bring to the boil. Lower heat and simmer until the sauce has been reduced by about one-quarter.

Just before serving, add the pickles and cook for about 1 minute. Serve hot with cooked meats, primarily pork.

Makes about 375 ml (12 fl oz/1½ cups).

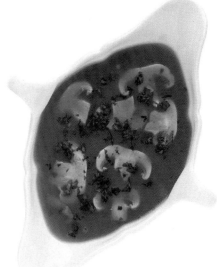

SAUCE CHASSEUR

250 g (8 oz) mushrooms
3 tablespoons butter
½ tablespoon vegetable oil
Salt and pepper
2 teaspoons finely chopped spring onion
2 tablespoons brandy, if desired
125 ml (4 fl oz/½ cup) dry white wine
250 ml (8 fl oz/1 cup) Sauce Espagnole, page 16
2 tablespoons Tomato Sauce 2, page 21
1 teaspoon very finely chopped fresh parsley

Wash and dry mushrooms; discard the stalks and thinly slice.

In a small, heavy-based saucepan, melt butter and add the oil. Sauté the mushrooms until they begin to turn light brown. Add salt and pepper, spring onion and brandy, if desired. Cook over low heat for 1 to 2 minutes, then add the wine and simmer until liquid is reduced to little more than half.

Add Sauce Espagnole and Tomato Sauce and parsley. Heat until bubbly. Pour into a serving dish and serve hot with grilled or roast meat, chicken or rabbit.

Makes about 375 ml (12 fl oz/1½ cups).

SAUCE DIABLE

2 spring onions
125 ml (4 fl oz/½ cup) dry white wine
125 ml (4 fl oz/½ cup) red wine vinegar
60 g (2 oz) butter
30 g (1 oz/¼ cup) plain flour
250 g (8 fl oz/1 cup) Brown Stock, page 8
Pepper
Pinch of cayenne pepper
2 teaspoons finely shredded fresh herbs (parsley, chervil, tarragon)

Finely chop the spring onions. Place in a medium saucepan and add the wine and vinegar. Simmer over moderate heat until the liquid is reduced to about 60 ml (2 fl oz/¼ cup). The onions should be very soft. Meanwhile, melt butter in a saucepan; stir in flour and cook about 10 minutes, stirring occasionally, until flour begins to brown. Add the Brown Stock and whisk together into a smooth sauce.

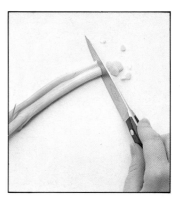

Add the stock mixture to the onions. Bring to the boil and cook for 5 minutes.

Strain spring onions through a fine metal strainer. Add black and red peppers to the sauce, then stir in herbs. Put into a sauce-boat and serve hot with grilled steaks or chicken breasts.

Makes about 500 ml (16 fl oz/2 cups).

Note: Some like a hotter sauce than this; add 1 tablespoon or more Worcestershire sauce when adding the wine and vinegar.

SAUCE MEUNIÈRE

125 g (4 oz) butter
1 tablespoon lemon juice, or more according to
   taste
About 2 tablespoons finely chopped fresh parsley
Fresh parsley sprigs
Lemon wedges

In a heavy-based saucepan over moderate heat, melt the butter and allow to turn lightly brown.

Add lemon juice and parsley. Serve hot, spooned over grilled fish with parsley sprigs and lemon wedges.

Makes 125 ml (4 fl oz/½ cup).

LEMON-BUTTER SAUCE

250 g (8 oz) butter
3 to 4 tablespoon lemon juice
2 teaspoons Worcestershire sauce
Pepper
2 tablespoons chopped fresh parsley or snipped
   fresh chives

In a heavy-based saucepan, melt butter. Add lemon juice, Worcestershire sauce and pepper. Simmer for about 1 minute, then add herbs. Serve hot spooned over grilled fish.

Makes 250 ml (8 fl oz/1 cup).

SUZETTE SAUCE

125 g (4 oz) butter
125 g (4 oz) sugar
1 orange
3 tablespoons orange-flavoured liqueur

In a heavy-based saucepan, melt the butter, then stir in sugar.

Using a citrus zester, add about 2 teaspoons finely shredded orange rind, then add about 1 tablespoon orange juice and the liqueur. Bring to the boil; lower heat and cook for 1 minute.

Serve from heated jug over fresh fruit or ice cream.

Makes about 375 ml (12 fl oz/1½ cups).

CRÊPES SUZETTE
Place sauce in a large frying pan. Add a pre-cooked crêpe and warm through; fold into quarters and push to side of pan. Repeat with remaining crêpes. Add 2 to 4 tablespoons more liqueur and set alight. When flames die down, serve crêpes with remaining sauce spooned over.

CHOCOLATE SAUCE

125 g (4 oz) plain chocolate
315 ml (10 fl oz/1¼ cups) milk
Vanilla essence, to taste
1 teaspoon sugar
4 egg yolks, well-beaten, room temperature

Chop or cut chocolate bar into pieces.

In a heavy-based small saucepan, heat milk, chocolate, vanilla essence and sugar over low heat until chocolate melts, stirring continuously. When liquid is just bubbling round edge of saucepan, remove pan from heat. Spoon a small amount of the hot liquid into the yolks, then add yolks to chocolate. Return to heat and continue stirring for 2 to 3 minutes without simmering, until thickened.

Serve hot with poached pears, ice cream, steamed puddings or soufflés.

Makes about 375 ml (12 fl oz/1½ cups).

FRESH RASPBERRY SAUCE

1 kg (2 lb) raspberries
1 tablespoon arrowroot
2 teaspoons orange or lemon juice
3 tablespoons sugar
Cream for decoration

Place berries in a food processor or blender and purée. Press through a fine strainer and discard seeds.

Mix arrowroot with a little of the juice; and set aside. Pour balance of juice into a heavy-based saucepan and add the sugar and orange or lemon juice. Heat slowly to dissolve the sugar, stirring constantly. Bring just to the boil, remove from heat and stir in arrowroot mixture. Lower heat, return to a simmer, stirring, and continue to cook for 1 to 2 minutes or until sauce is smooth and thickened.

Cool to room temperature. Spoon the sauce over bottom of serving plates. Carefully form a thin circle of cream round edge of sauce. Use a fine-pointed skewer to 'pull' cream in opposite directions at 2.5 cm (1 in) intervals.

Makes about 500 ml (16 fl oz/2 cups).

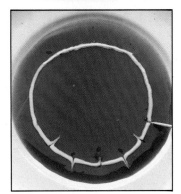

CUSTARD SAUCE

3 tablespoons Vanilla Sugar, see below
4 egg yolks
500 ml (16 fl oz/2 cups) milk, warm or scalded

Beat Vanilla Sugar and egg yolks together until light pale, smooth and creamy.

Add warm milk, stirring constantly. Transfer to top of a double boiler over barely simmering water.

Continue cooking, stirring, until sauce is thick enough to coat back of metal spoon; check frequently because the sauce can curdle if overcooked. Serve hot with desserts, such as fresh fruit pies.

Makes about 500 ml (16 fl oz/2 cups).

VANILLA SUGAR
Place three 7.5 cms (3 in) vanilla beans upright in a screw-top jar. Cover with sugar. Seal and leave for at least 1 week until the flavour has time to blend.

— CUSTARD SAUCE VARIATIONS —

BRANDY SAUCE
Remove Custard Sauce from heat; stir in at least 2 tablespoons brandy, whisking constantly. Serve hot with sliced fruitcake, ice cream or fruit salads.

Makes about 500 ml (16 fl oz/2 cups).

COFFEE-LIQUEUR SAUCE
Remove Custard Sauce from heat; stir in 2 tablespoons cold strong black coffee and 1 tablespoon coffee-flavoured liqueur, whisking constantly. Serve with ice cream, sweet cookies and chilled soufflés.

Makes about 500 ml (16 fl oz/2 cups).

RASPBERRY SAUCE
Remove Custard Sauce from heat; stir in at least 2 tablespoons strained raspberry purée, whisking constantly. Serve with gelatine moulds, ice creams or fresh fruit salads.

Makes about 500 ml (16 fl oz/2 cups).

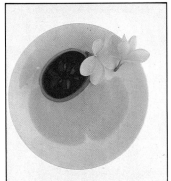

COFFEE & RUM SAUCE

125 ml (4 fl oz/½ cup) hot strong black coffee
2 teaspoons sugar
2 egg yolks
75 ml (2½ fl oz/⅓ cup) double (thickened)
   cream
1 teaspoon cornflour
1 tablespoon milk
2 tablespoons dark rum

Place coffee in the top half of a double boiler. Stir in sugar until dissolved, then cool slightly. Add egg yolks, one at a time, combining thoroughly after each addition. Have hot water just below simmering point in the bottom half of the double boiler, and heat coffee mixture.

Stir in cream and cook for 1 to 2 minutes.

Mix cornflour with milk, then add to saucepan and stir constantly until sauce thickens. If serving hot, add rum, stir and serve immediately. If serving cold, allow to cool, stirring occasionally to prevent skin formation. Add rum just before serving. Serve with fresh fruit.

Makes about 250 ml (8 fl oz/1 cup).

Note: As a variation, you can add coffee-flavoured liqueur in place of the rum.

RHUBARB-BERRY SAUCE

250 g (8 oz) rhubarb
250 g (8 oz) strawberries, hulled
125 g (4 oz/½ cup) sugar
Juice of 1 lemon
1 teaspoon finely grated lemon rind

Cut rhubarb into 5 cm (2 in) pieces. Place in a saucepan with water to cover and cook over moderate heat for 10 minutes, or until tender. Strain, discarding the cooking liquid.

Reserve a few strawberries for decoration. Place berries, rhubarb and remaining ingredients in food processor and purée.

Press through a fine strainer, then discard seeds and any stringy pieces of rhubarb. Cover and chill until ready to serve. Place in a serving dish with reserved sliced berries and serve cold with ice cream or crêpes.

Makes about 250 ml (8 fl oz/1 cup).

CARAMEL SAUCE

250 g (8 oz/1 cup) sugar
About 125 ml (4 fl oz/½ cup) water
1 strip lemon rind

In a heavy-based saucepan over moderate heat, cook sugar and water without stirring until sugar is dissolved. Add lemon rind. Continue heating for 4 to 5 minutes or until caramelization begins and sauce looks golden brown.

Have ready a saucepan of iced water and set the saucepan in it to cool quickly. This is important, otherwise the cooking process will continue and the syrup will have a burnt flavour.

Stir to cool with wooden spoon, then remove lemon rind. Serve cold.

Makes about 250 ml (8 fl oz/1 cup).

Note: Instead of lemon you may use orange rind, or add some brandy or Madeira just before serving. Ginger wine is nice, too.

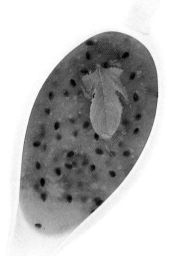

PASSIONFRUIT COULIS

6 passionfruit
2 tablespoons sugar
4 tablespoons water

Cut passionfruit in half crossways. Scoop passionfruit pulp, with seeds, into a small saucepan.

Add sugar and water.

For a thin coulis, heat until sugar has dissolved. For a thicker sauce, heat mixture to the boiling point. Lower heat and allow sauce to reduce to desired consistency. Serve hot or cold with poached fruit or ice cream.

Makes about 125 ml (4 fl oz/½ cup).

— Marmalade-liqueur Sauce —

125 g (4 oz/⅓ cup) marmalade, such as orange,
  lime or tangerine
2 teaspoons water
1 teaspoon lemon juice
2 tablespoons Grand Marnier or other
  orange-flavoured liqueur

In a small heavy-based saucepan,
combine the first 3 ingredients.

Bring to the boil over moderate heat.
Lower heat and simmer over low heat for
1 to 2 minutes, stirring occasionally.

Remove from heat. If serving hot, stir in
the liqueur and serve at once. If using
warm, cool to desired temperature, then
stir in the liqueur. Serve with crème
brûlée, poached fruit or a steamed
pudding.

Makes about 500 ml (16 fl oz/2 cups).

CHERRY COULIS

250 g (8 oz) cherries, fresh or stoned canned
60 ml (2 fl oz/¼ cup) water, or juice from
   cherries
3 tablespoons orange juice
1 tablespoon lemon juice
2 tablespoons sugar

If cherries are fresh, cook in water to cover over moderate heat until falling off the stones, then drain. If canned, drain, reserving 60 ml (2 fl oz/¼ cup) of the juice.

Place in a small saucepan with juice or water and add orange and lemon juices. Heat until warmed through.

Press through a fine strainer into a bowl. Stir in sugar while still hot and stir until dissolved. When ready to serve, re-heat over low heat. Serve with crêpes, soufflés, ice creams or sorbets.

Makes about 250 ml (8 fl oz/1 cup).

LEMON SAUCE

1 tablespoon arrowroot
About 6 tablespoons freshly-squeezed lemon
  juice
180 ml (6 fl oz/¾ cup) cold water
60 g (2 oz/¼ cup) sugar
1 lemon

In a small bowl, add arrowroot. Mix a little lemon juice with a little water and add to arrowroot. Beat to a smooth paste.

In a saucepan, heat remaining lemon juice and water. Add sugar, stirring constantly, until dissolved. Pour on to arrowroot paste, beating until smooth.

Return to saucepan over low heat, stirring constantly, until thickened and clear. Using a zester, add the rind of 1 lemon. Serve hot with slices of fruit pies and tarts and ice creams.

Makes about 250 ml (8 fl oz/1 cup).

Spicy Honey Sauce

150 ml (5 fl oz/²⁄₃ cup) maple syrup
75 ml (2½ fl oz/⅓ cup) honey
½ teaspoon ground allspice
1 teaspoon ground cinnamon
Pinch of caraway seeds

Mix syrup with honey in a small, heavy-based saucepan over low heat while stirring.

When sauce is hot, add spices and cook over moderate heat, stirring, until the sauce boils.

Serve hot from a heated jug with crêpes, bananas or waffles. Cool to warm, if serving with ice cream.

Makes about 250 ml (8 fl oz/1 cup).

Note: Always use the proportions ⅓ honey to ⅔ maple syrup.

BUTTERSCOTCH-ALMOND SAUCE

125 g (4 oz) butter
375 g (12 oz/2 cups) light brown sugar
125 ml (4 fl oz/½ cup) double (thickened) cream
2 teaspoons lemon juice
2 tablespoons chopped, blanched, toasted
   almonds

Melt butter in the top half of a double boiler over simmering water.

Add sugar and heat, stirring until sugar has absorbed butter. Add cream and carefully stir in lemon juice. Cook over barely simmering water for ½ to ¾ hour, stirring frequently.

Add chopped almonds. Serve hot over ice cream.

Makes about 500 ml (16 fl oz/2 cups).

Note: Chopped pecans or walnuts make pleasant variations.

HARD SAUCE

125 g (4 oz) unsalted butter
90 g (3 oz/¾ cup) icing sugar
Flavouring to taste, see below

In a bowl, cream butter until soft; slowly add sugar and beat until creamy and fluffy. Add flavouring of choice.

Spread on piece of aluminium foil; chill until firm. Cut into pieces for serving.

For a festive touch, pipe into rosettes: spoon sauce into a piping bag fitted with a star nozzle; pipe 5.25 cm (2½ in) rosettes on to a sheet of aluminium foil. Open freeze on foil, then transfer to a rigid container and layer with sheets of aluminium foil. Freeze for up to 6 months. To serve, transfer to refrigerator for ½ hour.

Makes about 315 g (10 oz/1¼ cups).

VARIATIONS:
There are endless possibilities for flavourings. For example, add a few drops vanilla, 1 or 2 tablespoons brandy or rum, or 2 tablespoons of your favourite liqueur. Add the flavouring gradually, beating constantly to avoid curdling.

— PINEAPPLE-LIQUEUR SAUCE —

125 ml (4 fl oz/½ cup) unsweetened pineapple
  juice
45 g (1½ oz/¼ cup) light brown sugar
60 ml (2 fl oz/¼ cup) water
2 teaspoons arrowroot
60 ml (2 fl oz/¼ cup) Benedictine liqueur
1 slice canned pineapple cubes
1 tablespoon finely chopped walnuts
6 stoned dates, chopped
Pinch of allspice
½ tablespoon butter

In a heavy-based saucepan, heat juice
and sugar over low heat, stirring
occasionally.

Meanwhile, blend water with the
arrowroot. Add to saucepan. Stir over a
moderate heat until sauce begins to
thicken. Increase heat and bring to the
boil. Lower heat, add all remaining
ingredients, except the butter, and stir
for 1 to 2 minutes.

Add butter; stir to melt. Serve hot with
steamed puddings, poached fruit or
vanilla ice cream.

Makes about 375 ml (12 fl oz/1½ cups).

— Apricot & Cognac Coulis —

125 g (4 oz) dried apricots
250 ml (8 fl oz/1 cup) water
1½ to 2 tablespoons sugar
1 teaspoon arrowroot
2 teaspoons water
60 ml (2 fl oz/¼ cup) Cognac

In a small heavy-based saucepan, cook apricots with the 250 ml (8 fl oz/1 cup) water and sugar for 5 to 7 minutes or until soft; the liquid will reduce slightly. Remove apricots and reserve liquid.

Mix arrowroot with the 2 teaspoons water. Add to saucepan with apricot liquid and cook over moderate heat, stirring, until the liquid thickens and clears. Transfer to a food processor or blender with the apricots and purée.

Return apricot purée to saucepan. Add Cognac and heat without boiling. Serve hot.

Makes about 315 ml (10 fl oz/1¼ cups).

Note: Individual preference will dictate sweetness (increase or reduce sugar), consistency (thin with boiling water if desired), and the amount of Cognac that suits your taste.

ZABAGLIONE SAUCE

8 egg yolks
125 g (4 oz/½ cup) sugar
250 ml (8 fl oz/1 cup) Marsala

In top half of a double boiler, beat egg yolks and sugar until thick and frothy.

Add Marsala and whisk in. Place over simmering water in bottom half of double boiler. Make sure the water does not touch the bottom of the top half. Cook, whisking constantly with an electric beater on moderate speed, until mixture thickens and doubles in volume. It should have a fluffy texture. Serve hot with fresh fruits, soufflés, steamed puddings or apple or banana fritters.

Makes about 500 ml (16 fl oz/2 cups).

CHILLED ZABAGLIONE:
To serve the sauce as a dessert, remove Zabaglione from heat when it has reached the fluffy stage. Pour into a bowl and place in a large bowl of water and ice. Stir gently until cool. Transfer to serving dishes and refrigerate until required. *Serves 4.*

Charcuterie Sauce, page 99, with pork
fillets, julienne carrots and spinach
noodles

Chilli Sauce, page 59, with deep-fried
prawns and boiled rice

Green Fish Curry, page 52, with boiled
rice

Bigarade Sauce, page 31, with roast duck

Italian Green Sauce, page 38, with
steamed white fish fillets

Velouté Sauce, page 12, with grilled
chicken breast and green beans

Fresh Raspberry Sauce, page 105,
with whipped cream

INDEX